MARCO ⊕ POLO

Insider Tips

D1077407

NEW ZEALAND

PAPUA
NEW GUINEA   SOLOM.

Coral   VANUATU
Sea   FIJI

New
Caledonia (F)   PACIFIC
OCEAN
AUSTRALIA   ○Brisbane

Canberra○   ○Sydney   NEW ZEALAND
○Melbourne

Tasman   ○Wellington
Sea

Tasmania   Chatham
Islands (NZ)

www.marco-polo.com

SYMBOLS

INSIDER TIP	Insider Tip
★	Highlight
● ● ● ●	Best of ...
☼	Scenic view
🌿	Responsible travel: fair trade principles and the environment respected

PRICE CATEGORIES HOTELS

Expensive	over 180 NZ$
Moderate	110–180 NZ$
Budget	under 110 NZ$

The prices are for two people in a double room without breakfast

PRICE CATEGORIES RESTAURANTS

Expensive	over 30 NZ$
Moderate	20–30 NZ$
Budget	under 20 NZ$

The prices are for a standard meal without drinks

On the cover: Paddle through the Abel Tasman National Park p. 109 | Freefall jumps from Sky Tower p. 37

CONTENTS

Trips & Tours → p. 106

Sports & Activities → p. 112

Travel with kids → p. 116

Road atlas → p. 132

DID YOU KNOW?

Timeline → p. 12
Local specialities → p. 26
Books & Films → p. 45
Pretty chilly → p. 49
In Tolkien country → p. 86
The Home of Bungee → p. 94
Currency converter → p. 126
Budgeting → p. 128
Weather in Wellington
→ p. 129

MAPS IN THE GUIDEBOOK

(134 A1) Page numbers
and coordinates refer to
the road atlas
(0) Site/address located off
the map. Coordinates are
also given for places that are
not marked on the road atlas
Maps of Auckland,
Christchurch, Dunedin and
Wellington can be found inside the back cover

**INSIDE BACK COVER:
PULL-OUT MAP →**

PULL-OUT MAP 𝄝

(𝄝 A–B 2–3) Refers to the
removable pull-out map

The best MARCO POLO Insider Tips

Our top 15 Insider Tips

INSIDER TIP **Polynesia pure**
For body and soul: at the market in Otara, a suburb of Auckland, you can immerse yourself in a little but authentic bit of exotic Polynesia → p. 37

INSIDER TIP **An idyll to dream in**
That pioneering feeling: set among fields, Puhoi keeps the memory of the first settlers from Bohemia alive → p. 39

INSIDER TIP **Driving on the wild side**
The 'Forgotten World Highway' (SH 43) winds its way through a bizarre landscape with Whangamomona village republic in the middle → p. 44

INSIDER TIP **Adventures in the Underworld**
If you want to explore the secret 'lost world' of the Waitomo Caves with their underground waterfalls, you'll have to endure one or other trial of courage → p. 60

INSIDER TIP **Nostalgic river trip**
The historic paddle steamer cruises down the Whanganui River, 'The Rhine of Maoriland' → p. 61

INSIDER TIP **Bizarre volcanic desert**
Tongariro Crossing: an exciting day's hike close to still active craters. A Maori chieftain once gave this national park to the British Crown → p. 63

INSIDER TIP **Twinkling lights**
From the lookout on Mt. Victoria, Wellington's local mountain (196m/ 643ft), the view takes in the whole city and the harbour. If you go up in the evening, New Zealand's capital is a sea of lights spread out at your feet → p. 63

INSIDER TIP **A bite with a view**
In Poseidon in the pretty little resort of Sumner near Christchurch you can enjoy breakfast, lunch or tea right on the sea – pure bliss → p. 74

BEST OF ...

FOR FREE

● *Free view from a crater*
On *Mt. Eden*, an almost 200m (660ft)-high extinct volcano, Auckland spreads out below you. This free 360° panorama is a real experience after dark when the city is transformed into a sea of lights → p. 35

● *Cold sea, hot springs*
No money needed here, just a bit of time. At *Hot Water Beach* on Coromandel Peninsula the earth turns on the hot tap at low tide and geothermal spring water bubbles up through the sand. Just dig a dip and let youself be warmed up → p. 40

● *Public WC as a work of art*
In *Kawakawa*, using the public convenience comes with an art experience free of charge. A New Zealander by choice, Friedensreich Hundertwasser put his artistic talents to a good use → p. 52

● *Steep, steeper, the steepest*
With an incline of 35°, *Baldwin Street* in Dunedin is the steepest residential street in the world. Residents should really charge an entrance fee as there as so many people who come here and drive up and down all the time. You don't need to do this. Instead, hold a race such as the *Baldwin Street Gutbuster* (photo below) → p. 76

● *Natural wonder*
These rock formations like layered pancakes on the west coast never cease to amaze. An there is no ticket office – only the lashing waves stop you from taking a closer look at the *Pancake Rocks* → p. 85

● *Step back into prehistoric times*
In many places, such things would be in a museum. Not so in the Catlins where a mass of petrified trees remains for all to see off the coast – but only at low tide can you marvel at this fossilised prehistoric forest that is more than 180 million years old → p. 78

●●●● Dots in guidebook refer to 'Best of ...' tips

ONLY IN NEW ZEALAND
Unique experiences

● *Art Nouveau par excellence*
In *Napier* you should definitely stroll around the attractive streets – a unique journey back through the history of design to when Art Nouveau was also all the rage as an architectural style too. No other town in the world can boast such a complete and consistent adherence this one building style → **p. 47**

● *The birthplace of New Zealand*
Visit the pretty place where the State of New Zealand was born: on the dramatic coastline with a view of the enchanting Bay of Islands. The *Waitangi Treaty Grounds* have been preserved as a kind of open-air museum today where the eventful beginnings of the nation are kept alive → **p. 50**

● *Maori folklore*
You can get a good insight into the Maori culture in Rotorua where New Zealand's first immigrants hold large Polynesian performances. The culinary highlight of this folkloric event with dancing and singing is the *hangi* – a feast of traditional delicacies cooked in an earth oven and served in generous portions → **p. 56**

● *Bird paradise on the edge of town*
Albatrosses spend most of their time in the air. On Otago Peninsula near Dunedin you can get a rare look at these magnificent birds at one of the few mainland colonies where the albatross chicks hatch in January/February (photo above) → **p. 80**

● *Rock hard and unique*
Every souvenir made of *greenstone* is a piece of New Zealand for back home. This type of jade is found exclusively on the west coast. In Hokitika, the centre of the greenstone trade, you can find both mass-produced articles and exquisite pieces of jewellery → **p. 86**

● *Courage on a rope*
Bungee jumping is a Kiwi invention: leaping into nothing with just an elastic rope fixed to an ankle attachment to stop you. In and around the adventure playground of Queenstown there are many places you can jump from, even from a height of 134m (440ft) at the *Nevis Bungee* → **p. 94**

ONLY IN

BEST OF ...

AND IF IT RAINS?
Activities to brighten your day

● *Among the sharks*
On Auckland's waterfront you can dive into the undersea world of the Pacific Ocean with its sharks, manta rays and colourful coral fish and still keep your feet dry – thanks to the glazed tunnel in the gigantic aquarium in *Kelly Tarlton's Underwater World* → p. 118

● *Kiwi kindergarten*
Kiwi Encounter is the name of the rearing station in Rotorua that gives a helping hand to the young of a very special bird, helping to ensure that more of these flightless and almost blind feathered friends will be found roaming the forests → p. 55

● *Disappearing off the face of the earth*
In *Waitomo Caves* (photo left) glowworms light up the faces of all cave explorers regardless of the weather. But you can get wet even underground if you go *black water rafting* on inflated tyre tubes → p. 60

● *The whole country under one roof*
Everything you ever wanted to know about New Zealand can be found in *Te Papa National Museum*, beautifully situated on the harbur bay in Wellington. You can spend hours here looking at the excellent displays → p. 64

● *To the South Pole and back*
Visit the icy continent without frostbite or snowstorms. The *International Antarctic Centre* in Christchurch creates a fascinating link to Scott Base on the South Pole → p. 73

● *Head scratching*
Puzzling World in Wanaka will cause your head to spin a bit with lots of optical illusions, the 'Pyschic Challenge' and various intriguing puzzles which can only be solved if you think logically → p. 100

RAIN

●●●● Dots in guidebook refer to 'Best of ...' tips

RELAX AND CHILL OUT
Take it easy and spoil yourself

● *The romance of the paddle steamer*
Prettily restored, *historic paddle steamers* depart on relaxing river cruises where the wide, slow-moving Whanganui River nears the estuary, passing peaceful, undisturbed scenery as far as the eye can see → **p. 61**

● *Geothermal therapy*
What bubbles up from the centre of the earth in and around Rotorua is good for the body and soul. Take a mud bath, a hot jet massage or simply relax in the geothermal pools → **p. 55**

● *Lunch among the vines*
An idyllically situated winery (photo below), an inviting terrace and excellent food are the best ingredients for a wonderful and envigorating lunch. Do as the locals do and book a table at *La Veranda* on the *Domain Georges Michel* estate in Marlborough → **p. 93**

● *Candlelit bathtubs*
'Candlelight package' are the magic words which turns a visit to *Onsen Hot Pools* near Queenstown into an incredibly romantic evening. With the glittering southern stars above and flickering candles around your private pool – what more could two people in love need to be happy? → **p. 96**

● *Unter a canopy of stars*
You can almost reach out and touch the stars at *Observation Point* on Stewart Island. A perfect place for the romantic at heart. Nowhere else in the country can you see the Southern Cross constellation better on a clear night than here → **p. 100**

● *Peaceful nights on the fjord*
You can only really experience the famed silence of Milford Sound in Fiordland if you spend the night out on the water in the fjord. Why not try an *overnight cruise* with all creature comforts on board one of the ships? → **p. 105**

INTRODUCTION

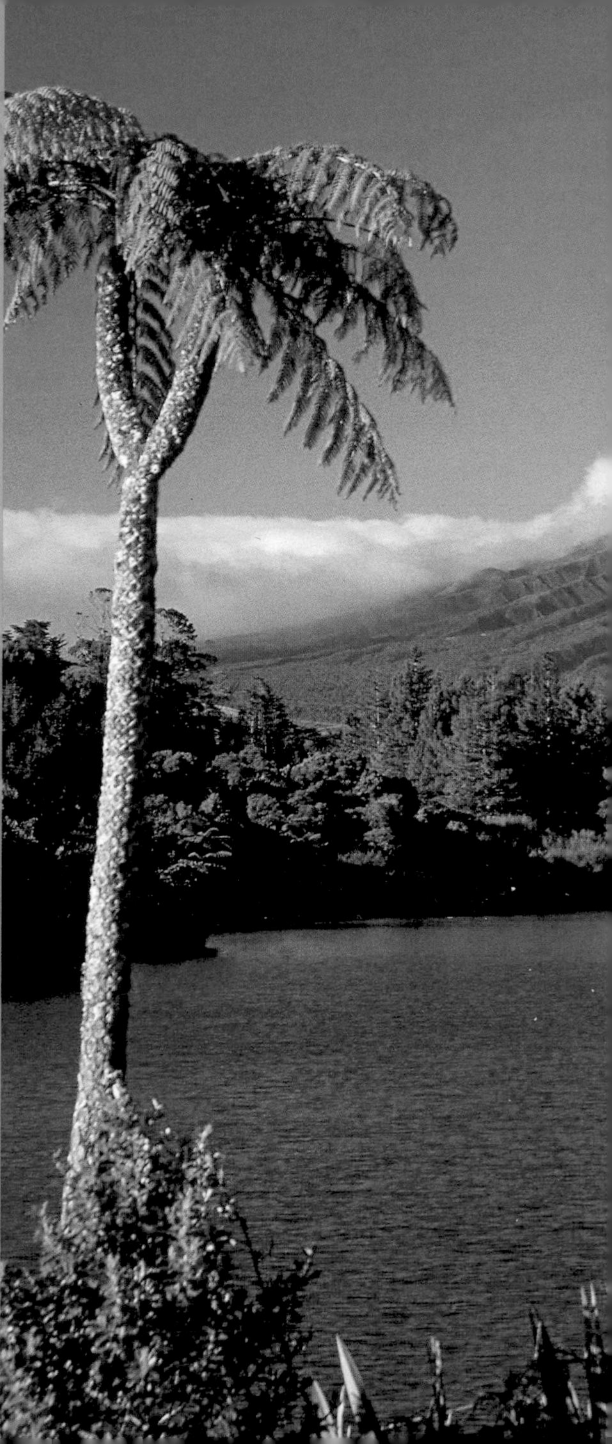

DISCOVER NEW ZEALAND!

A word of advice to start with: don't ever say that New Zealand is 'somewhere near Australia'. Firstly, the two landmasses are, after all, separated by a more than two-and-a-half hour flight. Secondly, the rivalry between the two nations can sometimes take on strange forms, even if it's not always meant seriously. It's bad enough that the kiwi (New Zealand's emblem), of all creatures, is reputedly descended from the Australian emu rather than the long-extinct New Zealand moa. The Aussie, according to the mocking Kiwi (of the human variety), is the uncouth descendant of British convicts who settled on the continent in 1788. Kiwis on the other hand, replies the Aussie, are simply afraid that their island state could slip off the bottom right-hand corner of the map for ever. And their even greater fear is that nobody will notice.

Their existence on the fringe of world events is taken by New Zealanders with a bit of self irony. They call themselves Kiwis after the endemic, half-blind, flightless and rather plump bird. Some 40 million sheep and 4.4 million inhabitants share North Island,

Photo: Mt. Taranaki on North Island

Where politicians are as busy as bees: Wellington's 'Beehive' with the adjoining parliament building

4.4 million people share the country with 40 million sheep

South Island and Stewart Island in the far south. The distance from top to bottom is approx. 1700km (1060mi); the surface area 103,500mi² – slightly larger than the UK which covers 95,000mi². If one were to dig a hole between France and Morocco through the centre of the earth, one would – theoretically – come out in New Zealand.

Not only a strip of water, Cook Strait, separates the two main islands. The wealthier, more densely inhabited North Island is worlds apart from the economically poor

ca. 925
According to Maori tradition, Kupe, a famous Polynesian seafarer, reaches the islands.

Researchers say the first settlers arrived between 1280–1300 AD. During this period, Polynesians (Maori) reach Aotearoa, 'the land of the long white cloud', in large canoes. They came from legendary Hawaiki, the whereabouts of which remains unknown

1642
Abel Janzoon Tasman claims New Zealand for Holland. He names it 'Staten Landt' which is later changed to 'Nieuw Zeeland'

but, from a scenic point of view, far richer South Island. The metropolis of Auckland, where – statistically speaking – almost every third New Zealander lives, is on North Island. And so is the capital city, Wellington, even if it is on the very southern-most promontory. South Island, with its 'major cities' Dunedin and Christchurch can barely counter that.

Geologically speaking, New Zealand is a 'newcomer', having risen from below the seas just 100 million years ago. The earth, by comparison, is some 4.7 billion years old. The fact that, deep down, powerful tremors are unleashed from time to time is due to the earthquake zone in which New Zealand is located. In 1931, seismic activity levelled the towns of Napier and Hastings, killing more than 250 people. An earthquake in early 2011 devastated the city of Christchurch. That there is still a lot going on in the centre of the earth can be seen in many places on the surface. Extensive geothermal activity can be found in and around Rotorua, and on the Coromandel Peninsula hot water even filters up through the sand on one of the beaches. The volcano Mt. Tarawera near Rotorua last erupted in 1886 and obliterated a whole village – now an open-air museum known as 'The Buried Village'.

> **Geologically speaking, New Zealand is a 'newcomer'**

New Zealand is really a peaceful corner of the earth. There are no dangerous wild animals. You can hike through the jungle as safely as if you were taking a Sunday stroll through a public park anywhere else. Criminality may have increased over the

1769
On 9 October the explorer James Cook lands near today's Gisborne and claims the islands for King George III

1840
On 6 February, the Treaty of Waitangi is signed by the *Pakehas* (Whites) and the Maoris, in which the Maoris accept British sovereignty and hand over land to the settlers, while being given the privileges of British citizens. At this time, the New Zealand Company buys Maori land to sell it to British settlers – a contentious issue to this day

1947
New Zealand is granted independence from Great

past few years in major cities but, compared to the rest of the world, New Zealand is still a little bit of paradise.

> **Environmental awareness is still not part of the Kiwis' everyday life**

The way they treat their environment, however, is not as it could be. The Kiwis limp along behind other western countries with regard to environmental protection. That's surprising, especially considering that an environmental party was founded in Wellington way back in 1972 – at that time, it was the only one in the world. Since 1990 the Green Party that emerged as a result has been represented in parliament. Its fight for a clean, green environment in the South Pacific has not been without inconsiderable success, managing to put a stop to mining projects and extending the boundaries of nature reserves and national parks. It is only in everyday life that the Kiwis' environmental awareness has not been given greater priority. Most simply do not have the money to buy a new reduced-emission car or to install solar panels on the roof or double glazing. As a result of prolonged dry periods during the summer, especially on South Island, however, everybody has at least now realised that the country's energy supply – most of which is generated by hydro-electric plants – is not endless.

Most tourists to New Zealand do not expect large cities, culture or a rich history, but a natural paradise on earth – and they are seldom disappointed. Where else can you find that? Broad, white, South Sea-like sandy beaches where you can dream away all on your own, a luxuriant mixture of green and flowering vegetation, thrilling hiking trails through the mountainous Southern Alps, far from civilisation, and chirpy birds, some of which have lost the ability to fly through a lack of natural enemies, and whose song makes ornithologists' hearts beat faster. Only the numerous sea creatures in the South Pacific need to fear over enthusiastic deep-sea fishermen.

Spring, summer, autumn, winter – New Zealand lives from season to season. In July, skiers take to the snowy slopes in the Southern Alps around Queenstown and Wanaka while the temperatures in the subtropical north of North Island are still pleasant. Summer, around Christmas and New Year, is the high season when Kiwis head for the water with children, charcoal, a boat and fishing gear in tow. Scenic stretches of the coastline change overnight into campsites – if holiday homes have not already got there first.

Britain while remaining a member of the Commonwealth

1985
The government declares the country to be the first nuclear-free zone in the world

2008
The national hero, Sir Edmund Hillary who, in 1953, was the first person to climb Mount Everest, dies in Auckland aged 88

2011
Almost 200 people die in the terrible earthquake in Christchurch. A large part of the city centre has to be rebuilt; the damage runs to more than 12 billion NZ$

Where else can you find this? Empty beaches such as at Wharariki near Farewell Spit

Another of the New Zealanders' passions is caring for their recent history. A 150-year-old house attracts amazed visitors who even pay an admission fee. Don't be taken in by the use of the word 'museum'. Sometimes this may be little more than a junk room with all sorts of different things that should really be turned out. On the other hand, some collections in tumble-down barns show a devoted attention to detail.

In 1999, the election of the Labour Party under Helen Clark brought political change. The equal rights of the Maoris' have since been established by law and the protection of their interests is given considerable importance – especially by the Labour Party

Christmas is high season when the Kiwis head for the seaside

but also by the conservative National Party that, with the support of Maori representatives among others, is now in power. Nevertheless, the number of Maoris on social benefits or unemployed is still disproportionately high.

It is a long time since New Zealand was considered one of the wealthiest nations in the world. An employee's average annual income today is around 30,000 NZ$. Many New Zealanders have to take on second jobs. That makes it even more admirable how Kiwis cope with everyday life: with a lot of improvisation while still enjoying the natural paradise on the doorstep.

The intact natural environment is also the New Zealanders' trump card. Almost 2 million tourists explore the islands at the end of the world every year – either by car or campervan, by mountainbike or on foot. And they are more than welcome!

WHAT'S HOT

1 Barley, hops, aniseed?

Beer Some breweries in New Zealand tend to ignore the purity law, but not to their disadvantage. The beer concocted by the *Invercargill Brewery* contains coriander, honey and passion fruit – and tastes delicious *(8 Wood St., Invercargill)*! Lemons, for example, find their way into the vat at the *Three Boys Brewery (Christchurch, www.threeboysbrewery. co.nz)*. Oat flakes and even chocolate are added to the stout and spices to the rye beer at the *Renaissance Brewing Company (1 Dodson St., Blenheim, photo)*.

Hula hoops

2

Tone your abs Get that hula hoop spinning! It strengthens your muscles and keeps you supple – and it's fun. Auckland's *Performing Arts School* holds 'Hip Hoop' courses *(100 Motion Rd.)*. If you've got time, sign up for an 8-week 'In 2 Hula' course *(www.hulahoops. co.nz)*. At *hoopla!* Michelle Keenan organises hoop 'jam sessions' outside *(Auckland, www.hoopla.co.nz)*. And at *Hoopnotica* you can get all you need, from DVDs to hoops, for that workout at home *(www.hoopnotiapprox. co.nz, photo)*.

3 Works of art

Graphic novels Comics are art. Mathew Tait from Christchurch has proved this with his black-and-white strips *(www.mattait.com)*, as has his prize-winning colleague Ant Sang whose 'Dharma Punks' series can also be found in galleries *(www. antsang.co.nz, photo)*. Exciting newcomers are ferreted out by *Cherry Bomb Comics*. Personal experiences are often the subject of graphic novels; super heroes are the exception *(www. cherrybombcomics.co.nz)*. Rarities can be found at *Comics Compulsion (12 Penelope Place, Christchurch)*.

Surf on wood

4

Eco-surfing Those on the crests of the waves off New Zealand don't use any old boards. They virtually all dream of Mike Grobelny's designs. His boards made of bamboo have even converted the surfing pro Luke Hughes. The elaborate decorations and carvings are a real eye-catcher *(www.mikegrobelny.blogspot.com, photo)*. Almost as popular are Roger Hall's wooden creations. Whoever can afford it, can have a surfboard made to measure *(8 Kepa Rd., Ruakaka, www.surfline.co.nz)*. David Farrar and Sean Newton at *Big Woody* beaver away on your behalf and create boards to order in paulownia wood from sustained plantations. If you register in advance, you can also test a whole range of boards *(19 a Portside Drive, Mount Maunganui)*.

Bedding down

5

Eccentric So you didn't sleep a wink? That happens to a lot of guests in their first night in *Woodlyn Park*. You'd simply be missing out on too much! The two hotels on the site are no normal hostels, but a propeller plane and a Hobbit cave *(1177 Waitomo Valley Rd., Otorohanga, photo)*. For some tourists, staying the night in *The Boot* is a dream come true. The hotel in Tasman is in the shape of a shoe. But this model isn't really suitable for the catwalk *(320 Aporo Rd.)*! Some 30 mins. from Christchurch you can bed down in a luxury Romany gypsy caravan without having to do without a TV or a queen-sized bed *(Wagonstays, 2115 Old West Coast Rd., Selwyn)*.

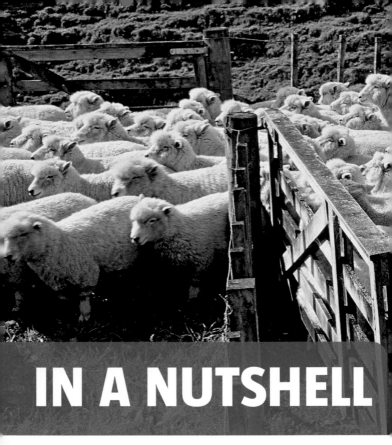

IN A NUTSHELL

CYCLING

For some time now cycling has been one of the New Zealanders' most popular sports – with the emphasis definitely on the word 'sport'. Cycling down under has less to do with it being a time-saving or ecologically-correct mode of transport but more with physical training – a kind of mass movement swept along by the continuing fitness fad. Thousands leap into the saddle and work hard at improving their stamina. You'll find virtually no touring bikes anywhere, but all the more aerodynamic racing and all-terrain mountainbikes. At the end of the working day and at weekends, roads and tracks are firmly in the hands of speeding enthusiasts in skin-tight sports gear and with the compulsory helmet on their heads. So be careful whenever you stroll across a seemingly little-used road!

ENVIRONMENTAL AWARENESS

The lack of environmental awareness is – in the natural paradise of New Zealand, of all places – unfortunately a common phenomenon. There are too many smoky chimneys and too many old cars polluting the air, too many front gardens, parks and grassy areas that use up the water reserves in hot summers. And most

Photo: For every New Zealander there are slightly more than nine sheep

Where Christmas trees are decorated in summer and birds cannot fly: a few oddities from 'the land of the long white cloud'

houses are still built as if energy saving through better insulation were a pure luxury. Everyone knows that things can't go on like this. But until the last Kiwi has been convinced about environmental protection and stops burning his garden rubbish in the open, will still take some time.

At least the government is moving in the right direction with its comprehensive catalogue of regulations and sanctions. And even supermarkets are reducing the availability of free plastic bags bit by bit. Nevertheless, there are a few pioneers down under who are directly targetting the environmentally-minded New Zealand tourist. 'Eco-friendly places to eat, stay and explore in New Zealand' are listed under ☺ *www.organicexplorer. co.nz.*

FARMING

New Zealand is often called the biggest farm in the world. Approx. 65,500mi² are used for agriculture, to grow crops or as grazing land for cattle, sheep and deer. Some 27,000 sheep farmers are major landowners who cannot even reach the remote parts of their land on foot. Venison has been exported to Europe since the 1960s when deer were first reared on farms. In the meantime, there are around 4000 deer farms with at total of 2 million animals.

Another key export is fruit. The pièce de resistance must surely be 'the world's finest kiwifruit' although many farmers do not make the profit they had hoped for. Planting, harvesting and shipping the delicate kiwis is hard work and cost intensive. New Zealand's apple farmers profit from the shift of the seasons. In the European winter and spring they can fill the supermarkets' shelves with freshly picked apples.

FAUNA

Although it may not be particularly pretty, is semi-blind and unkempt, the *Brown Kiwi* is the best looked-after bird in New Zealand. It is one of a total of five species that have lost the ability to fly due to the lack of natural enemies and is protected even though it is not threatened with extinction. The same goes for the bluey-green *takahe* (rather like a moorhen) and the night parrot – the *kakapo*. Many of the 250 species of bird in New Zealand are endemic, such as the *tui* and the *kea*. The latter is definitely the cheekiest bird – a green alpine parrot with a sharp beak that shows no respect for the rubber door linings of cars or windscreen wipers. Whereas *moas* (huge flightless birds) have become extinct, imported animals such as red deer, weasels and possums have bred in huge numbers due to the lack of natural predators. As a result they are now hunted – especially the possums that clear out whole flowerbeds.

The coastal waters are still rich in fish, large and small. In season, whales appear. Inland waterways are teeming with life and are richly blessed with gleaming rainbow trout. Two species of bat are the only endemic land mammals. One of the oldest species of animal in the world still lives in New Zealand: a genus of the order of lizard-like reptiles, the *tuatara*, has inhabited the earth for 200 million years.

FLORA

The variety of ferns that grow naturally can best be seen in the New Zealand bush, a dense jungle labyrinth with a temperate subtropical climate. There are almost 200 different types of fern, some of which can reach heights of up to 15m with leaves as long as 3m. In the mid 18th century, two thirds of the country was covered in thick forest; today it is less than one third. The *kauri*, a protected genus of tree, is rarely found today in New Zealand's woodlands. Imported trees such as the pine have spread much faster to the detriment of endemic species such as the *rata* or the *pohutukawa* – New Zealand's Christmas tree – that conjures up the right festive spirit with its bright red flowers in late December.

FRIDAY EVENINGS

Friday evenings is when the nightlife down under goes off the rails. Alcohol consumption rockets, not only in the pubs and bars but also at parties and events. Binge drinking has unfortunately also got the better of young too. In some of the more infamous watering holes, where people booze beyond reason, drunken guests often have a fisticuffs with others as the evening draws on. Avoid such pubs at all cost. And keep off the roads in the inner city areas, as Friday is when the 'hoons' are out and about: young drivers in souped-up, low-suspension cars zooming around town with screeching engines. The police keep an eye on things but seldom intervene.

GEOLOGY

Some 230 million years ago, when Australia was already a landmass, New Zealand lay under the sea. More than 100 million years still had to pass before the islands were to emerge above the surface of the water thanks to volcanic activity and tectonic movement. Glaciers carved out the landscape during the Ice Age and left clear traces: fjords, elongated lakes and moraines. Volcanic and geothermal activity still effect and alter the landscape today. Three quarters of the surface area are more than 200m (656ft) above sea level and the peaks on South Island top the 3000m (9850ft) mark. For more information on volcanoes and earthquakes see: *www.geonet.org.nz*

IMMIGRANTS

Immigrants have populated the originally uninhabited islands of New Zealand since time immemorial. First came the Maori, then immigrants from all over the world – most of them from Great Britain and Ireland. Today, almost 75% of New Zealanders are of European extraction, tendency sinking. Instead, the proportion of ethnic groups from Asia is growing rapidly. More than 10% already come from Asia; that's 35% more than from the Pacific region (South Sea Islands). New Zealand would like to be the melting pot of different cultures but the Chinese and Koreans in particular find integration difficult.

MAORI

Around 620,000 people in New Zealand call themselves Maori. Exactly where the Polynesians came from more than 1000 years ago is unknown. They themselves claim to be from *Hawaiki,* a

Wonderful Maori carvings in the meeting house in Waitangi Treaty Grounds

country enshrouded in mystery like Atlantis, that was probably in French Polynesia (near the island Raiatea). In simple, narrow, wooden canoes they travelled thousands of miles across the ocean before reaching *Aotearoa,* 'the land of the long white cloud', as New Zealand is called in the pictographic language of the Maori. The *iwi*, the tribe, was the largest entity that the Maori knew at that time. At its head was the chieftan, the *ariki*, who did not make decisions on his own. *Marae* (meetings) were held in the middle of the village and the head of each family could give his opinion. Trading was commonplace between tribes.

In the 19th century, more than 500 Maori tribes shared North and South Island. With the arrival of white settlers, countless Maori were carried off by imported diseases alone. At the time of the signing of the Treaty of Waitangi on 6 February, 1840, which granted the Maori the privileges of British citizens – at least on paper – and protected their lands, there were 100,000 Maori and only some 1000 European settlers in New Zealand. 18 years later, the whites were already in the majority. An aggressive settlement policy but also dissent among the Maori tribes rendered the treaty ineffectual, even though it was surprisingly forward-looking for the colonial period. Maori and *Pakeha* (Whites) have now been living in harmony side by side (as opposed to together) for many years. The Whites and dark-skinned New Zealanders have remained a nation of alienated neighbours in many respects, even though there are no racial restrictions and no discrimination. Nevertheless, the Maori are worse off than the white population in many areas: they account for the majority of unemployed and those dependent on social security. A large proportion of the younger generation, however, endeavours to support the state in establishing a new Polynesian self-awareness, called *Maoritanga*. The language and culture are being re-activated, but only one fifth of Maori speaks the native tongue. The pursuit of ownership and competitive thinking are not necessarily foreign to Maori, and their lifestyle barely differs from that of the white population. See: *www.maori.orgnz.tikanga*

NATIONAL PARKS

The 14 national parks in New Zealand cover almost 11,500mi² – 10% of the total area. In addition, there are three maritime parks around the coast and other protected areas, so that a total of 35% of country's territory is a conservation area. Only hikers are allowed to penetrate deep into the remote countryside on trails of varying difficulty and length, on the provision that they leave nothing behind except footprints.

Only hikers are allowed into protected areas such as the Mt. Cook National Park

OPEN HOME

Whoever simply wants to see how New Zealanders live should take advantage of the opportunity when a property for sale can be visited at set times. Don't feel inhibited when you see an 'Open Home' notice outside a house. Other people look by, especially on Saturdays and Sundays, mostly out of pure curiosity. The least are serious potential buyers. The price of property has rocketed over the past few years to such an extent that many people can no longer afford a home of their own. Seen in relation to income, houses in Auckland – according to one survey – are more expensive than in New York. Up until now, generations of Kiwis have trustingly put their money in a home, especially as a form of security in old age. The young in the larger cities are being left empty handed. On top of this, afford-able property to rent is rare.

POLITICS

The majority of Kiwis are no longer royalists, although few admit it. And so the country continues to be a member of the Commonwealth with the Queen as Head of State.

But just to make sure this is not misunder-stood: New Zealand happily operates as a sovereign, independent state. At the last-but-one parliamentary election, the prime minister at that time, Helen Clark (Labour Party), handed over leadership to the conservative John Key (National Party) after nine years in power. Key heads a centre-right minority government which also comprises the Maori Party, among others, and was re-elected in November 2011 with a wide margin. More than a dozen parties stand for election each time. When particularly important decisions have to be made for the country, referen-dums are also held.

FOOD & DRINK

The Brits dictated what was put in the pots for long enough – to the chagrin of many a gourmet who had every reason to decry the New Zealand variation of the much maligned English cuisine in the 1980s. Leathery steaks are now – fortunately – a thing of the past.

The New Zealand cuisine has gained considerably in taste, not least of all thanks to the aid of countless foreign chefs. Local produce is of exceptional quality. Just think of all the dishes that can be made of tender lamb. Beef is often and gleefully eaten as a steak: fillet, rump or sirloin vary in tenderness and price. Rib eye (tenderloin) fillet is particularly juicy. The plate-sized T-bone steak is best for those with a huge appetite! Venison comes from local deer that, virtually tame, are reared in herds on farms. However the meat tends to lack that typical taste of wild deer. The New Zealanders themselves are wild about chicken, either roasted chicken breast or drumsticks in bread crumbs. Chicken in all sorts of different varieties fills the shelves of little self-service take-aways or coffee shops at lunchtime, where imaginatively made snacks ranging from sandwiches to filled rolls and pies can also be found.

The day kicks off with just one thing: an English breakfast where you can fill up on eggs and bacon, sausage and/or fish and

Photo: Typical – fish and seafood specialities

Tasty lamb, crayfish and Bluff oysters feature a lot on New Zealand's menus which, over the years, have become much more varied

hash browns. Lunches are often cold but healthy with masses of different green vegetables and bean shoots. Many New Zealanders are real health fanatics.

Immigrants from around the globe have expanded the gastronomic delights on offer. Small very good Chinese restaurants can be found almost everywhere, the Italians are slowly daring to produce more than just lasagne and cannelloni, the French generally run the gourmet temples, and the countless Japanese tourists make a bee-line for the sushi bars with their morsels of raw fish.

Blue cod, red snappers and local hoki can be found without heads and already filleted in fish shops. Prepared in this way, they soon find their way into the deep-fryer to be wrapped up in paper in fish-and-chip shops and eaten on the hoof.

LOCAL SPECIALITIES

▶ **afternoon tea** – often served with (current) scones, jam and cream
▶ **blt** – bacon, lettuce and tomato are the initials of the three ingredients used to garnish hamburgers or found in the respective sandwiches
▶ **latte** – popular milk coffee (one third espresso, two thirds hot foamy milk), often served in a paper beaker 'to go' (photo left)
▶ **muffins** – warm bites between meals, either savoury and spicey or fruity and sweet (photo left)
▶ **mussel patty** – greenshell mussels baked in bread crumbs
▶ **oaky** – name of a wine that has matured in small oak barrels. Similar to oak (or barrique) wines in Europe
▶ **oysters kilpatrick** – oysters cooked with diced bacon
▶ **pavlova** – sugary-sweet dessert that looks like the stiff tutu of the Russian prima ballerina of the same name

▶ **pumpkins** – there's hardly a soup served in New Zealand in late summer and autumn without pumpkin. But it can taste different from time to time thanks to the variety of eastern and western recipes used
▶ **sandwiches** – the traditional English snack has fired the imagination of those down under and is available with virtually every conceivable filling that can fit between two slices of bread – often toasted and cut diagonally to be eaten as finger food
▶ **seafood chowder** – a light-coloured, creamy and filling seafood soup (photo right)
▶ **silverbeet** – chard has been grown by the Maori as a crop for a long time
▶ **steak & kidney pie** – often served as a hearty snack rather than something to make a gourmet's heart beat faster
▶ **tuatua fritters** – a fried mussel dish, once a favourite of the Maori, that is rarely found on a menu today

1kg of oysters from the Pacific can be bought in little plastic bowls at one of the oyster farms in the Bay of Islands for around 15 NZ$. Bluff oysters, named after the town on South Island, are only available from the end of March until August. Greenshell mussels (also called green lipped mussels) are rather like common mussels but almost twice the size. They are cheaper and sold in plastic bags. Without their shells, smoked for a longer shelf-life and sea-soned with a variety of spices, mussels are often eaten as a snack between meals. You don't need to go without crayfish even if you're on a shoestring budget. The bright red delicacy is usually sold in various sizes, pre-cooked and ready to eat. Little stalls around Kaikoura and in Whitianga (Coromandel Peninsula) are good addresses. When New Zealanders fancy something small, they pick on whitebait – the tiny, transparent young of the common galaxia. Whitebait fritters are like omelettes but can be a bit tasteless.

You can live hand-to-mouth, so to speak, from New Zealand's richly filled fruit basket. Apart from various kinds of apples and pears, nashis – a juicy cross between a pear and an apple – as well as cheap avocados and kiwis are equally tempting. Fancy a sweet potato? The Maori of old used to cooked the kumara in their earth ovens – a method regularly celebrated for tourists at *hangi* feasts in Rotorua.

As colonies of bees can busy themselves happily among the abundant blossoming vegetation, they produce an exquisite variety of honey in next to no time. Manuka honey, from the flower of the shrub of the same name, is very tasty. Manuka honey comes with a UMF or MGO classification. Scientific research has proven the honey's antibacterial potency (when used for external applications) – a shimmer of hope in the battle again bacteria resistent to antibiotics.

Riesling, Chardonnay, Cabernet-Sauvignon and Müller-Thurgau are grape varieties also grown on New Zealand soil. Dry or medium dry – low-priced cask wine in a 3-litre container is very popular and a good table wine. Sparkling wine (brut) has gained in quality. Hawke Bay and the Auckland region are known for their good red wines, Marlborough for its excellent whites. Try the kiwi wine too!

Beer drinkers should not be misled by German-sounding names. Beer is served English-style, full to the brim, without a head and served at the bar. The many little boutique breweries, called micro breweries, can be located using the reliable Internet site: *www.beertourist.co.nz*. The selection of fruit juices is also huge. Due to the flood of apples, the 'apple base' often accounts for 75% of the drink, i.e, even orange and

Cocktail time – preferably outside

cherry juice is three-quarters apple juice. A proper coffee-house culture has established itself, not least of all thanks to Italian immigrants. The *barrista* of today must master the full repertoire of the espresso machine. A sought-after expert who can do much more than simply make coffee, as Kiwis love to celebrate cappuccino & co.

SHOPPING

It's really not easy for visitors to New Zealand not to get tangled up in the wool of some 40 million sheep. High-quality knitware is produced using the very best merino wool from the highland farms on South Island (e.g. *Icebreaker*). For that luxurious feel close to your skin go for the mixture of merino wool and opossum hair, called *merino mix* (e.g. from *Untouched World*). For those after something more wind and weather-proof, try the heavy woollen bush shirt with large tartan patterns (e.g. from *Swanndri*), as worn since time immemorial by local shepherds.

GREENSTONE & GOLD

Greenstone is a semi-precious form of jade that owes its value to the stonecutters' skill. So-called greenstone factories, in Hokitika for example, flood the market with cheap but pretty stones. Artists create all sorts of little precious objects in all shades of green, often drawing on old Maori motifs. *Koru* (based on the unfurling frond of a fern) is popular, as is the *twist* (rather like intertwined knots) that are worn around the neck as *tiki* (amulets). A number of work-shops in Hokitika as well as the *Arts Centre* in Christchurch and the *Te Papa Museum Shop* in Wellington are reliable addresses for genuine greenstone jewellery. You can find that gleaming souvenir in one or other goldmine in New Zealand, such as small nuggets made into earrings or pendants.

MAORI CRAFTS

Carvings in wood and bone of traditional Polynesian motifs as well as basketwork and woven goods made of flax can only be found in New Zealand. High-quality sculptures and masks made by artists come at a price. The *Te Puia Arts and Crafts Centre* in Rotorua has a good selection. Souvenirs of a lifetime in the form of tattoos of Maori patterns have become fashionable. Small tattoo parlours offer their services on almost every street corner.

OUTDOOR CLOTHING

Before you deck yourself out with the right clothes for your trip through New Zealand's natural wonderland, remember

From woolly dreams to golden nuggets: stock up on pullovers, scarves and socks, green jade and semi-precious stones

that down under the selection is vast and the prices low. Numerous specialist shops offer a huge range of goods from the fashionable to the practical. Outdoor shops can be found in Auckland, Wellington, Christchurch and Queenstown, in particular. Around Easter, prices are cut. Excellent quality, made in New Zealand is guaranteed by the family-run company *Earth Sea Sky (www.earthseasky.co.nz)* in Christchurch.

PAUA & MOTHER-OF-PEARL

Cleaned and polished, the bright and shiny shell of the paua mussel makes a stunning table or room decoration. Ormer shells, as they are called in Britain, are also used for all sorts of jewellery items, but many earrings, amulets, bracelets and hairclips are not worth the money. If you look hard there are some lovely pieces amongst all the cheap rubbish, e.g. at *Pauanesia (35 High St.)* in Auckland. Mother-of-pearl jewellery almost always looks more exquisite, especially if it comes from Neil Hanna's workshop. Reasonably-priced works of art can be ordered online *(www.neilhanna. com)* or after visiting the studio in *Remuera* in Auckland *(tel. 09 5 24 75 16)*.

PELTS & LEATHER

All the different things that can be made from sheepskin can be seen in the souvenir shops, jam-packed with goods ranging from wonderful bedside rugs to dyed pink soft toys. Young fashion designers show what they can do with sheepskin and come up with trendy jackets and coats, including using the pelts of closely sheared young animals that are often turned inwards. Uggs – low sheepskin boots – are still hip and can be bought everywhere. Deerskins generally come from the local deer farms.

THE PERFECT ROUTE

AROUND THE NORTH

In **①** *Auckland* → p. 33 take a last whiff of city air before emersing yourself in the wonderful scenery of the north. Plan a detour along the **②** *Tutukaka Coast* → p. 39 lined with beaches. In **③** *Paihia* → p. 50 you can take in the beauty of the Bay of Islands around you and the historical places nearby. Guided jeep tours are offered for day-trips to the remote **④** *Cape Reinga* → p. 52 (photo left). State Highway (SH) 12 takes you westwards to imposing giant trees in **⑤** *Waipoua Kauri Forest* → p. 55.

IDYLLIC BEACHES AND HOT SPRINGS

After the longish tour to the south, enjoy the soft sand of the beaches on **⑥** *Coromandel Peninsula* → p. 40, where the thermal springs on *Hot Water Beach* will warm you up. Gourmets satisfy their hunger on oysters at the *Coromandel Oyster Company*. Further southwards is **⑦** *Rotorua* → p. 55 – a hotspot both for Maori culture and geothermal activity.

WILDERNESS AS FAR AS WELLINGTON

After *Lake Taupo* you reach **⑧** *Tongariro National Park* → p. 63. Exciting trails lead you through this upland volcanic region. Carry on parallel to the *Whanganui River*. At the southern point of North Island is the capital, **⑨** *Wellington* → p. 63. Cultural highlights include *Te Papa Museum* and culinary delights along *Courtenay Place*.

UNDER THE SOUTHERN SUN

The car ferry takes you across to the sunny north of South Island where you can head off straight away for the **⑩** *Marlborough Sounds* → p. 93, one of a labyrinth of deep bays that can also be explored on the Mail Boat. Back on dry land again, follow the *Queen Charlotte Drive* down the picturesque coastline of fjords. Beyond Nelson, turn off onto the SH 60 towards **⑪** *Abel Tasman National Park* → p. 89. Marahau is the starting point for fantastic hikes and kajak tours.

WILD WEST

Back on the SH 6, you will reach the bizarrely formed **⑫** *Pancake Rocks* → p. 85 to the west of the thundering breakers in the West Coast region. If you're looking for souvenirs, head for **⑬** *Hokitika* → p. 86,

Experience the different facets of New Zealand, from its northern-most tip to the far south, with detours to whales and volcanoes

where you can buy lovely jewellery made of greenstone – a type of jade. Further south, just take to the air: ⑭ *Franz Josef Glacier* → p. 81 and *Fox Glacier* → p. 82 are best seen on a sightseeing flight.

FOR ADVENTURERS
Beyond Haast Pass is ⑮ *Queenstown* → p. 93, one big playground with all sorts of thrills: *rafting, jet boats* and *bungee jumping*. And if you can't get enough, just take a plane from here to the famous *Milford Sound* and explore the fjord with its waterfalls and colonies of seals and penguins by boat.

STRANGE BOULDERS
Cross over to the east coast, to ⑯ *Dunedin* → p. 76 and to the *Otago Peninsula,* where penguins and albatrosses take to the stage (photo below). Further north near ⑰ *Moeraki* → p. 78 you can pick your brain on an unsolved mystery. The huge boulders on the beach have remained a puzzle to this day.

MOUNTAINS AND WHALES
Beyond Oamaru the roads lead to the Southern Alps. Right in the middle is the majestic ⑱ *Aoraki Mt. Cook* → p. 68, New Zealand's highest mountain. The route now follows the SH 1 again as far as ⑲ *Christchurch* → p. 71. If you like, take a train to ⑳ *Kaikoura* → p. 93, buy a helping of fresh crayfish and head off for a spot of whale-watching along the coast.

3850km (2390mi). Driving time: 76 hours. Recommended time for this trip: 4½ weeks. Detailed map of the route on the back cover, in the road atlas and the pull-out map

NORTH ISLAND

The question is always the same and answering it is equally difficult: on which island should I spend the most time? The scenery on North Island is perhaps not as breathtaking as on South Island with its magnificent mountains, romantic lakes and wild, rugged west coast. Nature-lovers should therefore plan a little more time for the south, but North Island also has its own unique scenery.

North Island, with the capital Wellington, is the country's economic engine and home to almost two thirds of a total of 4.4 million New Zealanders. When the rich cousins from North Island talk rather pityingly about their poor relatives in the south, the latter are quick to quote the image in Maori mythology of the demi-god Maui. Once, when out fishing in his canoe (South Island), he hooked a particularly fat fish (North Island) – the mouth of which is Wellington's natural harbour.

New Zealand's North Island – fine sandy beaches in the northeast around the beautiful Bay of Islands, a volcanic region and ski resorts in the middle, a rich fruit and wine-growing area in the east, and oil and natural gas fields in the Tasman Sea to the west. And those who can't do without city life will feel quite at home in the major urban centres Auckland and Wellington.

Beaches, volcanoes, large cites: for the Maori, a fat fish on a hook, for everyone else the economic heart of New Zealand

AUCKLAND

 **MAP INSIDE BACK COVER**
(136 B1–2) (ΩΩ H–J5) **Auckland has spread out like an octopus along the narrow 70km (43½mi) isthmus between the Pacific and the Tasman Sea.**

Almost every family here owns or lives in a house with a little garden. High-rises

---

CITY **WHERE TO START?**
Queen Street: The major commercial thoroughfare leads to the station and the waterfront and the gastronomic area of Viaduct Basin/ Princes Wharf. Other attractions can easily be reached by bus, e.g. on the circular *Auckland Explorer* route.

Who's watching whom? In the transparent tunnel at Kelly Tarlton's Underwater World

can only be found in the city centre. Today's leisure-orientated residents call Auckland the 'City of Sails', as every sixth resident has his own sailing boat in the harbour.

Auckland is the hub of New Zealand's economic activity. Of the more than 1.3 million inhabitants, a quarter are Maori or come from islands in the Pacific, mostly from Samoa and the Cook Islands. For this reason, Auckland is also known as the Polynesian capital of the world.

The city was founded in 1840 and was even the capital after Russell and before the seat of government was moved to Wellington in 1865. Since then, rivalry between the two cities has been great. The attention-seeking quarrelling always ends in a comparison of hours of sunshine and rainfall.

SIGHTSEEING

The *Auckland Explorer* bus passes 14 sites worth seeing including Victoria Market, Mission Bay, Parnell Village, Auckland War Memorial Museum and Sky Tower/Casino *(daily 9am–4pm)*. You can alight and have at least 30 minutes at each site (no guided tours included), before the next double-decker comes. *Ferry Building | Quay St. | day ticket 35 NZ$ | www.explorer bus.co.nz*

You can reach many of Auckland's tourist attractions more cheaply and with greater flexibility on the green *Link Bus (Discovery Pass 15 NZ$/day incl. North Shore ferry, tickets from the driver | www.maxx.co.nz).* The red *City Circuit* bus in the centre operates free of charge every 10 mins. *(daily 6am–11.30pm).*

AUCKLAND MUSEUM

For those not heading for the Bay of Islands, this museum will give you the opportunity to learn a lot about the history and culture of the Polynesians who first landed on the islands. 30-min. Maori cultural performances are held at 11am, noon and 1.30pm (Jan–April also 2.30pm, *approx. 25 NZ$). Auckland Domain | daily 10am–5pm | 5 NZ$ | www.aucklandmuseum. co.nz*

HAURAKI GULF

46 islands can be found in the gulf. *Waiheke* is a popular destination in the summer with its inviting vineyard gardens. Wonderful hikes take you through the thick vegetation on the volcanic island of *Rangitoto* (off Mission Bay). Information under *www.360discovery.co.nz.* The Pride of Auckland Company organises yacht tours around Hauraki Gulf and Waitemata Harbour *(Pride of Auckland Company | Viaduct Habour | tel. 09 3 73 45 57 | from approx. 60 NZ$ | www.prideofauckland. com, www.explorenz.co.nz).*

KELLY TARLTON'S UNDERWATER WORLD

A glass tunnel leads you through a fascinating undersea world. *Daily 9am–6pm, in summer 9pm | Orakei Wharf, Tamaki Drive | 34 NZ$ | www.kellytarltons.co.nz*

MOTAT

The original monoplane flown by the New Zealand aviation pioneer Richard Pearse (1877–1953) can be seen in the Museum of Transport and Technology. *Great North Rd. | daily 10am–5pm | 14 NZ$ | www. motat.org.nz*

MT. EDEN ☼ ●

From the 196m (643ft)-high former Maori fortified hill – *pa* in their language – Auckland's location on 60 volcanic hills becomes clear. The view at nightfall of the twinkling lights between Manukau and Waitemata Harbours is fantastic.

MARCO POLO HIGHLIGHTS

VOYAGER NZ MARITIME MUSEUM

Impressive exhibition of New Zealand's seafaring history in 14 halls. *Corner Quay/Queen St. | Hobson Wharf | summer daily 9am–6pm, winter 5pm | 16 NZ$, free if visited in combination with a trip on the Pride of Auckland | www.maritime museum.co.nz*

FOOD & DRINK

The monthly magazine 'Metro' lists all the 'in' places. The most up-market restaurants are on *Hurstmere Rd.* (Takapuna), *Parnell Rd., Ponsonby Rd.* and *Victoria Rd.* *(Devonport | www.northshorenz.co.nz)*, in *Viaduct Basin (America's Cup Village)* and along *Princes Wharf.*

HARBOURSIDE ☆

Enjoy freshly cooked fish in a gentle breeze on the terrace. *Ferry Building | lunch/dinner daily | tel. 09 3 07 05 56 | Expensive*

NON SOLO PIZZA

One of the best Italian restaurants in the city. *259 Parnell Rd. | dinner daily | tel. 09 3 79 53 58 | Budget–Moderate*

INSIDER TIP SWASHBUCKLERS

This popular fish restaurant lies right on the marina. If it's full, try the *Auckland fish market (22–32 Jellicoe St. | Freemans Bay | www.aucklandfishmarket.co.nz)*. The little stalls are a good alternative. *23 Westhaven Drive | lunch/dinner | tel. 09 3 07 59 79 | Budget–Moderate*

SHOPPING

DRESSMART

More than 40 outlet shops offering discounts of up to 70% compared to high street prices. Sometimes worth a visit, sometimes not. *151 Arthur St., Onehunga | bus 324, 334, 348 from downtown bus terminal, Customs St. East*

HIGH STREET

Running parallel to Queen St., this is the home of young, daring fashion designers, hoping for that career break.

KINGSLAND

This small district has advanced to become a favourite for modern Aucklanders with bars, restaurants and designer shops *(400–510 New North Rd., between Kingsland Ave. and Bond St.).*

LOW BUDGET

▶ Free maps are available from the *New Zealand Automobile Association* if you show your UK AA membership card *(Auckland | 99 Albert St. | tel. 09 3 02 18 25 | www.aa.co.nz).*

▶ A ☆ short trip round Auckland's *Waitemata Harbour* can be had on the ferry to Devonport: for less than 10 NZ$ *(return journey almost 30 mins. | from Ferry Building | Quay St.)* you have a wonderful view of Auckland's skyline.

▶ 4 and 5-star hotels in the capital Wellington have temptingly low rates at weekends when there are no business guests.

▶ If you pitch your tent on the campsite in *Waikite Valley,* 32km (20mi) south of Rotorua, you can use the traditional thermal spa next door free of charge *(signposted on the SH 5 | tel. 07 3 33 18 61 | www.hotpools.co.nz).*

INSIDER TIP **OTARA MARKET** ●

This large and lively market for fruit, vegetables and odds-and-ends provides an insight into the Polynesian heart of Auckland. *Sat 7am–noon | Otara | exit Hwy 1*

steep **INSIDER TIP** *Waitakere Ranges*, in *Piha* and *Karekare*. A point of interest: this is where the beach scenes in the prize-winning film 'The Piano', directed by Jane Campion, were filmed. You can also swim near *Muriwai*, where a colony of northern

Auckland's up-market dining district, Viaduct Basin, is right on the marina

PARNELL STREET & VILLAGE ★

This charming shopping district with its labyrinth of stores, has a Victorian air about it. This is where you'll find unique fashion items and can enjoy a relaxed cup of coffee or a break in one of the pubs. *www.parnell.net.nz*

VICTORIA PARK MARKET

Weekend flea market with a range of craft shops at other times.

LEISURE & SPORTS

SWIMMING

Beautiful beaches can be found on the West Coast, with sandy bays among the gannets breeds *(www.arc.govt.nz)*. For relaxing near the city head for *Mission Bay* and around *Takapuna*.

SKY JUMP/SKY WALK

Daredevils jump from the 192m (630ft)-high Sky Tower. The Sky Walk at the same height is above *Hobson/Victoria Street. Approx. 225 NZ$ /combi tickets 290 NZ$ | www.skyjump.co.nz*

HARBOUR BRIDGE EXPERIENCE ﹏

A 1½-hour climb up the 65m (213ft)-high Harbour Bridge gives you a wonderful view of the harbour and the city skyline. Even weddings have been held up here. Photography is however not allowed –

Head for the heavens: Sky Tower

but you can bungee jump if you like *(www. ajhackett.com)*. *100 NZ$ | tel. booking/ info 09 3 77 65 43 | www.aucklandbridge climb.co.nz*

RUNNING AND HIKING
If you want to train for the *Fun run round the bays* (always in March, 10km/6¼mi), you can run around *Mission Bay* to *St Heliers Bay*. The path from the Pacific to the Tasman Sea is however more interesting. Information on the more than 16km (10mi) *coast-to-coast walkway* can be found in the visitor centre or under *www. aucklandcity.govt.nz.*

ENTERTAINMENT

AMERICA'S CUP VILLAGE/ VIADUCT BASIN
The 'in' place for Kiwis and tourists to be is on the marina in the city centre *(Viaduct Basin/Princes Wharf)*. *Wynyard Quarter* and *North Wharf* that adjoin it are now developing into a residential and recreational area with restaurants and an outdoor cinema, reached via the Te Wero Bridge from Viaduct Basin.

SHAKESPEARE TAVERN BREWERY
Five beers from real ale to lager brewed on the spot on three floors and pulled along the lines of 'Two beers or not two beers, that is the question'. *61 Albert St. | daily from 11am*

SKY CITY CASINO
Tastefully decorated casino with restaurants, bars, a theatre and a good 4-star hotel. *Hobson/Victoria St. | open 24 hours*

SKY TOWER ☆
Auckland's landmark is exactly 328m (1076ft) tall and is really worth visiting both during the day and night. Good restaurants – the revolving *Orbit (Moderate–*

Expensive) with a view to die for is the cosiest, but you should book a table days in advance *(tel. 09 3 63 60 00). Hobson/ Victoria St. | daily 8.30am–11pm | www. skytower.co.nz*

WHERE TO STAY

AMITEE'S ON PONSONBY
Tastefully furnished B&B, many good restaurants and bars in the vicinity. *7 rooms | 237 Ponsonby Rd. | tel. 09 3 78 63 25 | www.amitees.co.nz | Moderate*

BASE ACB
(AUCKLAND CENTRAL BACKPACKERS)
300 beds in double and 4-bed rooms in the city centre (with a travel agency). Good place to head for if backpacking. *229 Queens St. | 3 floor | tel. 09 3 58 48 77 | www.stayatbase.com | Budget*

COPTHORNE HARBOUR CITY
With a view of the marina and Harbour Bridge. *188 rooms | 196 Quay St. | tel. 09 3 77 03 49 | www.copthorneharbourcity. co.nz | Moderate*

METROPOLIS
In the middle of the shopping district with a ☆ view of the harbour from the suites. *145 rooms | 1 Courthouse Lane | tel. 09 3 00 88 00 | www.hotelmetro.co.nz | Expensive*

INFORMATION

AUCKLAND I-SITE
Sky City (basement, at entrance to Sky Tower) | Corner Victoria St. and Federal St. | tel. 09 3 63 71 80 | www.aucklandnz.com

DEPARTMENT OF CONSERVATION
Information on national parks. *Ferry Building | tel. 09 3 79 64 76 | www.doc. govt.nz*

WHERE TO GO

KAWAU ISLAND
(136 B1) *(ш J4)*
An animal and plant paradise with wallabies and antilopes, as well as *Mansion House,* once the country home of the Governor Sir George Grey (1812–98). Day trips by boat leave from Sandspit *(near Warkworth north of Auckland | tel. 0800 11 16 16 | www.reubens.co.nz). 25km/15 mi north).*

INSIDER TIP PUHOI
(136 B1) *(ш H4)*
Some 65km (40mi) north of Auckland, Bohemian settlers set up home in Puhoi in 1863. Just off Hwy 1 and a few miles north of romantic Wenderholm Regional Park, the village has kept its pioneer character. *Puhoi Tavern* (dating from 1879), *Puhoi Cheese* (approx. 3km/2mi further on – the homemade cheese is a *must*) and *Puhoi Cottage* on the far edge of the village are worth a visit. Tip: homemade *berry muffins* in The Cottage *(Thu–Tue 10am–6pm).*

INSIDER TIP TUTUKAKA COAST
(135 D3) *(ш H–J3)*
A lovely stretch of coastline north of Whangarei with wonderful beaches and a classy marina. The gastronomic heart of Tutukaka Marina is *Schnappa Rock (breakfast, lunch, dinner daily | tel. 09 4 34 37 74 | Budget–Moderate).* The detour off the SH 1 can be recommended as a rewarding alternative route northwards – especially for sea-angling boat trips *(Yukon Charters | tel. 021 2 61 17 79 | www.yukon.co.nz).* The *Poor Knights Islands* nearby are a popular diving ground with a teeming underwater life between old shipwrecks *(Dive Tutukaka | Marina Rd. | tel. 09 4 34 38 67 or 0800 28 88 82 | www.diving.co.nz). 80km (50mi) north*

WHANGAREI
(135 D3) (*𝄐 H3*)

The gateway to remote Northland, with a population of 46,000, has inviting cafés and restaurants, especially around the central *Town Basin* and along the river banks. Refreshing beer without additives is served in *Brauhaus Frings (104 Dent St. | tel. 09 4 38 46 64)* with live music from local bands on Wed and Fri. A journey through time, literally, can be had at *Clapham's Clocks,* where 1400 clocks from various eras are on display *(daily 9am–5pm | Town Basin)*. If you want somewhere to stay, it is worth taking the twisty Whangarei Heads Road to *McLeod Bay,* where you can rent the *Breakaway Retreat,* superbly situated right on the sea. *(1856 Whangarei Heads Rd. | tel. 09 4 34 07 11 | www.breakawayretreat.co.nz | Expensive).* 140 km (84mi) north

COROMANDEL PENINSULA

(136 C1–2) (*𝄐 J–K5*) **This peninsula is a real natural wonderland in a small area with scrubland, mountains, woods and South Sea-like beaches.**

The biggest towns and places on the peninsula are Thames, Coromandel, Whitianga and Tairua, each of which offers a lot to see and explore.

SIGHTSEEING

GOLDMINE EXPERIENCE TOUR
This goldmine, restored using a lot of initiative and including an ore-crushing stamper battery, gives an authentic insight into the golden history of the peninsula *(Dec–March daily 10am–4pm | 10 NZ$ | Thames, corner Moanataiari Rd./ Hwy 25)*. Information: *Thames i-SITE | 206 Pollen St. | tel. 07 8 68 72 84 | www.thecoromandel.com, www.thamesinfo.co.nz*

LEISURE & SPORTS

SWIMMING
There are some lovely beaches on the Coromandel Peninsula: e.g. *Cook's Beach* in Mercury Bay or *Mare's Leg Beach* in Hahei where a footpath (further information under *www.tewhanganui-a-hei.org. nz*) takes you past *pohutukawa* trees to *Cathedral Cove,* a hidden beach with a portal-like arch through the cliff that is, however, closed at present. The small car park gets hopelessly overcrowded in summer!

A few miles beyond Hahei is ★ ● *Hot Water Beach* – a real 'hot' spot. Just dig your own nicely heated pool in the sand at low tide. The deeper you dig, the hotter it gets. Things are a big cooler when the tide is in.

Moko Artspace, a fascinating craft shop, is opposite the beach *(www.moko.co.nz)* and approx. 2km (1¼mi) from a large campsite *(www.hotwaterbeachholiday park.com | tel. 07 8 66 31 16 | Budget)*.

INSIDER TIP ▶ JOHANSEN ADVENTURES
Damian and Sharon run interesting tours to old goldmines, during which you can learn some practical things, such as what leaves can be used instead of soap or loo paper. Prices of tours depend on the destination and duration. *Pauanui Beach | tel. 07 8 64 87 31 | www.coromandel.co.nz*

WHERE TO STAY

GRAND MERCURE PUKA PARK RESORT
Particularly lovely resort with 50 chalets and two restaurants on a wooded hill, but without a view of the sea. Massages, Kneipp therapy, etc. available in the spa.

Do-it-yourself: just dig your own pool on Hot Water Beach

Pauanui Beach | tel. 07 8 64 80 88 | www.pukapark.co.nz | Expensive

HAHEI HOLIDAY RESORT
This campsite with cabins, motel rooms and holiday houses is right on a lovely sandy beach. Perfect for excursions in the area and for kajak tours. *Harsant Ave. | tel. 07 8 66 38 89 | Budget–Expensive*

WHERE TO GO ON THE COROMANDEL PENINSULA

COROMANDEL (136 C1) (*ȹ J5*)
This little place with its attractive colonial-style houses, pretty hotels, restaurants and souvenir shops has another trump card. This is where the potter Barry Brickell not only runs an interesting gallery but also a quirky narrow-gauge railway, the **INSIDER TIP** *Driving Creek Railway*. His dream: to have the railway that runs through the 70-acre Coromandel nature park lead to a natural history museum. The weird and wonderful 1-hour, 4km (2½mi),

return journey across a series of viaducts is quite an experience *(Kennedy Bay Rd. | daily 10.15am, 2pm, Oct–April also 11.30am, 12.45pm, 3.15pm and other times as necessary | 20 NZ$ | tel. 07 8 66 87 03 | www.drivingcreekrailway.co.nz)*. The **INSIDER TIP** *Coromandel Oyster Company* sells home-grown mussels *(daily | Tiki Rd. | 6km/3¾mi) to the south on Hwy 25)*. Information under *www.coromandeltown.co.nz*

INSIDER TIP KAUAERANGA VALLEY
(136 C2) (*ȹ J5*)
More than 20 hiking trails each taking several hours lead through the rugged wooded hills east of Thames. The prettiest day-trip is the 7–8 hour combination of the *Billygoat Circuit* and *Pinnacles*. Cabins and campsites provide accommodation for longer walks over several days. Impressive visitor centre at the entrance to the park *(tel. 07 8 67 90 80 | www.doc.govt.nz)*. Campervan pitches (no electricity) in natural surroundings in the park, 8km (5mi) from the visitor centre.

TAIRUA (136 C2) (*M K5*)
Located on a wide estuary, the village has developed into a compact shopping centre for the often lifeless holiday settlement of Pauanui opposite and the surrounding area. Several nice cafés, restaurants and shops are right on the main road. A number of different places provide comfortable accommodation. *Paku Lodge (30 rooms | 10 The Esplanade | tel. 07 8 64 85 57 | www.pakulodge.co.nz | Moderate)* is quietly situated and has a view across the water.

WAIHI (136 C2) (*M K5*)
During the goldrush on Coromandel from 1867–1907, gold to the total value of more than 3 billion pounds was found. An American company now mines approx. 100,000 ounces of gold in *Martha Hill Mine* every year. To do this, 3 million tonnes of rock are removed annually. Later, a recreational area is to be created to cover the scars of the 60-acre open-cast mine. *Guided tours Mon–Sat 10am and 12.30pm, approx. 2 hours | information centre daily 9am–5pm | viewing platform Moresby Ave. | tel. 07 8 63 90 15 | www.marthamine. co.nz, www.waihi.org.nz*
The nicest campsites are in *Waihi Beach* on the perfectly white sandy beach *(e.g. Bowentown Beach Holiday Park | 510 Seaforth Rd. | tel. 07 8 63 53 81 | www. bowentown.co.nz | Budget)*.

WHITIANGA (136 C1) (*M J5*)
Lovely beaches in the vicinity and a favourite place for sea-anglers. On top of this, it's also a place to indulge: freshly cooked crayfish for example are available in all fish shops and good restaurants down the esplanade. And if bad weather makes the beach less attractive, you can warm yourself up at the thermal pools in ● *The Lost Spring (daily 11am–8.15pm, im winter 6.30pm | 121 Cook Dr. | tel. 07 8 66 04 56 | www.thelostspring.co.nz).* The day spa offers treatments and massages as well as an excellent restaurant *(Moderate)*. Another possibility for a rainy day is to join an art course where you can learn how to carve items of jewellery from bone in the traditional Maori way *(Dec–March daily 10am–1pm | 12 The Esplanade | tel. 07 8 66 40 21 | www.baycarving.com).*
Whitianga has the widest selection of places to stay, some with sea views and correspondingly more expensive, e.g. *Beachfront Resort (8 rooms | tel. 07 8 66 56 37 | www.beachfrontresort.co.nz | Expensive)* or the centrally located *Oceans Resort (25 rooms | tel. 07 8 69 52 22 | www.oceans resort.co.nz | Moderate–Expensive).* Flats/ holiday homes for longer stays can be found under *www.bachcare.co.nz.* Information: *Whitianga i-SITE | 66 Albert St. | tel. 07 8 66 55 55 | www.whitianga.co.nz*

MT. TARANAKI

(136 A5) (*H8*) While crossing the green plain to the southwest, the volcanic cone of Mt. Taranaki – or Mt. Egmont as it is still marked on lots of maps of the area – can be seen from far away, usually covered with a white cap.

This area is a little off the beaten track. Apart from *New Plymouth*, the east side of Mt. Taranaki in particular is of interest to tourists. How the mountain came to be so isolated is described in Maori mythology as follows: after a dispute over a young, female mountain, Mt. Pihanga, the male rivals, Mt. Tongariro and Mt. Taranaki in the centre of North Island, quarrelled so much that Taranaki finally moved off and dug a long ditch (the Whanganui River bed), before the sea close by stopped him in his path.

SIGHTSEEING

MT. TARANAKI

Clouds usually hide the 2518m (8260ft)-high mountain peak, the sides of which are partly covered by dense forests up to the treeline. The 4-day *Round the Mountain Track* is popular among hikers. ☀ Approx. 17km (10½mi) from Stratford near *Mountain House Motor Lodge* on Pembroke Rd. is a viewpoint.

TAWHITI MUSEUM

All sorts of curiosities associated with the pioneering era have been collected by the artist Nigel Ogle and are displayed in a former cheese factory. The history of the

Poor old Mt. Taranaki: according to a Maori myth, the mountain is lonely and disappointed

region is presented in a variety of scenes with sometimes life-sized figures made by the extremely creative owner himself.

STRATFORD I-SITE

Broadway South | on the SH 3 | Stratford | tel. 06 7 65 67 08 | www.stratfordnz.co.nz

Forgotten World Highway? You won't even find anywhere to park in Taumarunui on the main road

Fri–Mon 10am–4pm (or by appointment) | 7 NZ$ | tel. 06 2 78 68 37 | Hawera | 40 Ohangi Rd. | www.tawhitimuseum.co.nz

WHERE TO STAY

ANDERSON'S ALPINE LODGE

Swiss chalet atmosphere and attentive hosts. *3 rooms | 922 Pembroke Rd. | Stratford | tel. 06 7 65 66 20 | Moderate*

INFORMATION

SOUTH TARANAKI I-SITE

Tower Grounds | 55 High St. | Hawera | tel. 06 2 78 85 99 | www.stdc.co.nz

WHERE TO GO

INSIDER TIP FORGOTTEN WORLD HIGHWAY (136 A–B5) (*M H8–J7*)

The 150km (93mi)-long road (SH 43) between Stratford and Taumarunui winds its way through enchanting hilly countryside with a lot of wilderness, few people and no petrol stations. 12km (7½mi) are still unsurfaced. A lovely half-day trip if you make a couple of stops en route, e.g. in *Whangamomona*, a sleepy place that nevertheless took the initiative and declared itself an independent republic and gained a lot of publicity. You can eat and sleep in *Whangamomona Hotel*

(11 rooms | 6018 Forgotten World Hwy | tel. 06 762 58 23 | www.whangamomona hotel.co.nz | Budget–Moderate), that has aged with dignity. A rural B&B with a small campsite and lovely views is 10km (6¼mi) further northeast *(Back Country Accomodation | Tahora | Forgotten World Hwy | tel. 06 762 58 58 or 0274 40 41 96 | Budget)*. Kajak and canoe tours over several days on the *Whanganui River* start from *Taumarunui (www.taumarunuicanoe hire.co.nz)*.

NEW PLYMOUTH (136 A5) (*ℳ H7*)

Off-shore gas and oil fields gave New Plymouth, 30km (18½mi) to the north, an economic boost back in the 1950s and again in the mid 1980s, when the production of synthetic petroleum was launched in Motonui.

A certain affluence can be detected here. There are some excellent restaurants such as fashionable ⚜ *Gusto* on the marina *(lunch, dinner daily | Ocean View Parade | tel. 06 759 81 33 | www.gustotaranaki. co.nz | Moderate)* and, next door, the fish specialist ⚜ *Galleon Bistro*, more rustic in style but perfectly located for the sunset *(Tue–Sun | tel. 06 757 43 22 | Budget–Moderate)*. In the centre, right on the showy waterfront, is the highly interesting *local museum (Mon/Tue 9am–6pm, Thu/Fri 9am–9pm, Sat/Sun 9am–5pm)* in the *Puke Ariki* complex *(1 Ariki St. | www.*

BOOKS & FILMS

▶ **An Angel at My Table** – autobiographical novel by the writer Janet Frame who died in 2004, describing, among other things, her time spent in a closed psychiatric institution following a diagnostic error. Filmed by the New Zealand director Jane Campion.

▶ **The Piano** – a film also directed by Jane Campion of a very unusual 19th-century love story. Told with impressive photography and set in the rainforests of New Zealand., the US actress Holly Hunter, who played the central figure, Ada, was awarded an Oscar in 1994 for her performance.

▶ **The Bone People** – a novel to get you thinking. Three lonely characters who struggle to come to terms with the loss of traditional family ties. With Maori blood in her veins, the authoress Keri Hulme, knows what she is writing about.

▶ **The World's Fastest Indian** – in this moving film from 2005, no-one less than Anthony Hopkins plays the obstinate Kiwi Burt Monroe, who dreams of setting a land speed record for motorcycles on his Indian Scout bike.

▶ **Whale Rider** – a socially critical film intertwined with Maori mythology. Released in 2002 is became an international box-office success. A 12-year-old Maori girl wants to become the chief of the tribe in the face of ancient traditions.

▶ **The Garden Party and Other Stories** – this volume of short stories by the New Zealand writer Katherine Mansfield is one of the classics of the 20th century. The anecdotes related by the authoress who was born in Wellington and died aged just 34 in France, are sprinkled with a generous portion of sarcasm.

The beautiful Art Deco buildings had a sad beginning: an earthquake destroyed old Napier

pukeariki.com) that also houses a café, restaurant and the i-SITE. Art-lovers will be enthralled by the exhibits in the *Govett-Brewster Art Gallery (daily 10am–5pm | 42 Queen St.)* that also has an impressive display of contemporary works by local artists. Good quality, modern crafts are available at *Kina NZ Design and Artspace (101 Devon St. West | www.kina.co.nz)*.
The town with its dark-coloured beaches shows its definitively prettier side in October and November when the ⭐ *Pukeiti Rhododendron Gardens* burst into flower *(2290 Carrington Rd. | 29km (18mi) from New Plymouth)*.
Tupare Gardens (Mon–Fri 9am–5pm, Sat/Sun 10am–3pm, summer only | 487 Mangorei Rd. | turning off Hwy 3, Broadway/Miranda St. | Stratford) and *Pukekura Park (daily 9am–7.30pm, Dec–Feb 11pm | Liardet St.)* are also awash with colour. The

colourful *Taranaki Rhododendron Festival* starts in November. Information: *New Plymouth i-SITE, Puke Ariki (in the foyer) | 1 Ariki St. | tel. 06 759 60 60 | www.new plymouthnz.com, www.taranaki.co.nz*

SURF HIGHWAY (SH 45)
(136 A5–6) (*ᗰ G–H 7–8*)
The SH 45, also known as *Surf Highway*, leads from New Plymouth to the dark-coloured by no less lovely sandy beaches and popular surfing places. Attractive sections of the coastline can be found just a little way off the 100km (62mi)-long stretch of road to Hawera, such as *Oakura (Oakura Beach Holiday Park | right on the sea | tel. 06 752 78 61 | www.oakura beach.com | Budget)* or the surfers' mecca *Opunake (Opunake Beach Holiday Park | tel. 06 761 75 25 or 0800 75 80 09 | www. opunakebeachnz.co.nz | Budget)*.

NAPIER

(137 D6) *(⬭ K–L8)* ★ ● **Napier (pop. 50,000) is regarded as one of the most beautiful Art Deco towns in the world and is a rare, homogenous architectural ensemble of the period.**

The story behind this, however, is a sad one. On 3 February, 1931, a massive earthquake devastated the towns of Napier and Hastings. After just 3 minutes, a large proportion of both towns had been reduced to rubble. 256 people died. Within 3 years a new town was built. The architects placed considerable value on retaining the Art Deco style. The geometrical ornamentation and shapes were symbols of the modern, unfussy period, free from old conventions.

SIGHTSEEING

ART DECO WALK

An informative leaftlet available from the i-SITE is a useful guide for the almost 1½-hour walk around the Art Deco town. **INSIDER TIP** In the evenings, the buildings are discreetly lit. Guided tours: *Deco Centre | 163 Tennyson St. | daily 2pm, approx. 2 hours*, from the *i-SITE | daily 10am, Jan–March also daily 5.30pm, approx. 1 hour | www.artdeconapier.com*

HAWKE'S BAY MUSEUM AND ART GALLERY

Very good audiovisual show on the history of the town. *Daily 9am–6pm | 65 Marine Parade | 7.50 NZ$ | www.hawkes baymuseum.co.nz*

NEW ZEALAND NATIONAL AQUARIUM

The aquarium with the adjoining Kiwi House provides an insight into the local undersea world. Swimming with the sharks is popular *(daily 9am, 11am and 3pm).*

Daily 9am–5pm | Marine Parade | 18 NZ$ | www.nationalaquarium.co.nz

WINE-GROWING ESTATES

The mild climate and the fertile soil make *Hawke Bay* famous for its wine and apples. It stretches from the Mahia Peninsula to Cape Kidnappers, with Napier as its main centre. Two of the dozen vineyards in the region are especially commendable: *McDonald Winery* has a small wine museum *(daily 9am–5pm, tours at 10am, 11am, 2pm, 3pm | 150 Church St.). Mission Winery* dating back to 1851 is the oldest in New Zealand *(Mon–Sat 9am–5pm | 198 Church St.).* Both vineyards are to the southeast in Taradale. Excellent lunches are available at *Mission* and also at *Te Awa (Hastings | 2375 Hwy 50 | tel. 06 8 79 76 02), Clearview Estate (Te Awanga | 194 Clifton Rd. | tel. 06 8 75 01 50)* and *Craggy Range (253 Waimarama Rd., on the road to beautiful Tuki Tuki Valley | tel. 06 8 73 71 26),* all *Moderate*.

FOOD & DRINK

INSIDER TIP **WEST QUAY/AHURIRI**

A choice of good restaurants and bars, some with terraces and seaviews, are located in former warehouses in the suburb of Ahuriri, some 3km (1¾mi) from the centre.

SHOPPING

CLASSIC SHEEPSKINS

Every year New Zealand exports some 230,000 tonnes of wool to 50 countries. One of the biggest warehouse districts is in Napier. At *Classic Sheepskins* everything from bedside rugs to soft toy dogs are sold and also mailed. The guided tour of the sheepskin factory is free. *Mon–Fri 7.30am–5pm, Sat/Sun 9am–5pm, guided tours (45 mins.) daily 11am, 2pm | 22*

Thousands of gawky gannets congregate every year in December on Cape Kidnappers

Thames St. | between the city centre and Westshore/harbour | www.classicsheep skins.co.nz

OPOSSUM WORLD
An exhibition on this cute but bothersome marsupial with a delightful souvenir shop. *Daily 9am–5pm | 157 Marine Parade | www.opossumworld.co.nz*

OCEAN SPA ☼
Lovely seaview from heated saltwater pools. *Mon–Sat 6am–10pm, Sun 8am–10pm | 42 Marine Parade | tel. 06 8 35 85 53 | www.oceanspa.co.nz*

WHERE TO STAY

BEACH FRONT MOTEL
Spacious rooms with sea views. Good value for money. *56 rooms | 373 Marine Parade | tel. 06 8 35 52 20 | www.beach frontnapier.co.nz | Moderate–Expensive*

INFORMATION

NAPIER I-SITE
100 Marine Parade | tel. 06 8 34 19 11 | www.isitehawkesbaynz.com

WHERE TO GO

CAPE KIDNAPPERS (137 E6) (*ØJ L8*)
With its wingspan of approx. 1.75m (5ft9in), the New Zealand gannet is the smallest of its species worldwide. The first young hatch at the beginning of Dec. The 10,000 yellow-headed birds that breed on the cape some 15km (9½mi) southest of Napier have got used to the 15,000 tourists and ornithologists who come here between Nov and June.

The starting point for this excursion is *Clifton Beach* (with two campsites). If you intend taking the footpath along the beach next to the cliffs (approx. 8km/5mi), do not leave Clifton earlier than 3 hours after high tide or the Cape not later than 1½ hours after low tide. Tide timetables at the i-SITE where you can also book tours to the colony (www.gannetsafaris.com, www.gannets.com). Te Awanga Motor Camp is a good base for campers and caravaners (Kuku St. | tel. 06 8 75 03 34) or Clifton Reserve, approx. 1.5km (1mi) further on, right on the sea (tel. 06 8 75 02 63).

GISBORNE
(137 F4) (*M7*)

Young Nick, a lad on James Cook's 'Endeavour', was the first English person to sight land here in 1769. In his honour, a promontory was named after him: 'Young Nick's Head'. At the turn of the millennium, every square inch on Mt. Hikurangi, a 90-minute drive further on, was taken up. Based on the the international date line, it is here that you can watch the first sunrise of a new day visible anywhere from the mainland.

Everything is wine-orientated here in and around the town as the climate and soil produce choice wines with which local wine-growers win prizes every year. If you prefer organic wines, try those at Milton Winery (Manutuke | 119 Papatu Rd.). A map of all vineyards can be found at the i-SITE (209 Grey St. | tel. 06 8 68 6139). 215 km (133mi) northeast

HASTINGS
(137 D6) (*K8*)

With Napier just 20km (12½mi) away, this town (pop. 70,000) is not just achitecturally at a disadvantage – the sea is also nowhere to be seen and most wine-producers are further away too. But it is still worth a quick visit, especially for gourmets. They have been coming here since 1926 to Rush Munro's (Mon–Fri noon–5pm, Sat/Sun 11am–5pm | 704 Heretaunga St. West) for the delicious homemade ice cream, the exquisite chocolates from the Silky Oak Chocolate Company (1131 Links Rd.) that melt in the mouth, the tasty cheese at Hohepa Organic Cheeses (363 Main Rd.) which they make themselves from the milk of naturally reared animals, as well as other organic delicacies. And children will love Splash Planet water theme park (p. 118).

PRETTY CHILLY

The sea around New Zealand seldom tops 18°C even at the height of summer. For your own safety, those who like it cool should however only swim or splash around on sections of the coast with lifeguards as the currents are dangerous. Attractive alternatives are hikes to lonely beaches where you should simply enjoy the fine soft sand. Many places along the 5650km (3510mi) coastline are like being in paradise. The most beautiful beaches on North Island: Ninety Mile Beach (Northland), Coopers Beach (Doubtless Bay), Hahei Beach (Coromandel Peninsula), Mount Maunganui (Tauranga) and around Raglan. On South Island, the best beaches stretch from Marlborough Sounds to Nelson, Abel Tasman National Park, and Golden Bay to Farewell Spit (Wharariki Beach).

HAVELOCK NORTH
(137 D6) (𝓜 K8)

This little town benefits from the extensive vineyards in the area. Wine-lovers and gourmets head for the wine-growing estates for lunch, e.g. *Black Barn (www.blackbarn.com)* or the ultra-modern *Craggy Range Vineyard (www.craggyrange.com)*. ☆ *Te Mata Hill* offers a wonderful view over the ecologically intact Tuki Tuki Valley and the wavy coastline of Hawke Bay. *Tom's Cottages (116 Matangi Rd. | tel. 06 8 74 79 00 | www.tomscottages.co.nz | Moderate–Expensive), 15km (9½mi) south-east* are two cosy places to stay in an idyllic location.

Waitangi Treaty Grounds: a mask on a Maori war canoe

UREWERA NATIONAL PARK
(137 D–E 4–5) (𝓜 K–L7)

The fourth largest national park in New Zealand. Its name means 'burnt penis'! The chieftan of a Maori tribe got too close to the fire one night while asleep and badly burnt this sensitive part of his anatomy. From *Wairoa (100km/62mi northeast of Napier)* it is 70km (44mi) to wonderfully peaceful *Lake Waikaremoana* (137 E4–5) (𝓜 L7) which has a campsite *(tel. 06 8 37 38 26)* and visitor information centre *(tel. 06 8 28 64 06 | www.lake.co.nz)*. The journey takes you past the most beautiful section of this very remote park which is home to the Tuhoe tribe, who have been given the name 'Children of the Mist'. The very twisty road from Wairoa to Rotorua takes at least 5 hours.

PAIHIA

(134 C3) (𝓜 H3) **Just less than 4 hours by car north of Auckland is the Bay of Islands, a mass of some 140 islands and islets around the little towns of *Paihia*, *Kerikeri* and *Russell*.**

The bay, with its long, light-coloured sandy beaches, is part of Northland. This region is not only historically interesting (3km/2mi north of Paihia, in *Waitangi,* is the 'birthplace of New Zealand'). It is also perfect for anglers, sailors and lazybones. The highest kauri trees, fruit plantations, a 90km (56mi)-lomg beach can all be found in the area with its wide variety of scenery.

SIGHTSEEING

WAITANGI TREATY GROUNDS ★ ●

The visitor centre at Waitangi Treaty Grounds gives a very interesting historical summary of the time New Zealand was settled.

The path from Treaty House leads through a mangrove wood past an impressive, 35m (115ft)-long war canoe for 150 warriors, made from the trunks of two kauri trees joined together. Every year, during *Waitangi Day* celebrations (6 February), it takes to the water again.

50 Maori chieftains and representatives of the British Crown under the Governor for New Zealand, William Hobson, assembled on the huge, well-tended lawns in front of Treaty House on 6 February, 1840, and sealed the Waitangi Treaty, in which the Maori handed land over to the settlers. A copy can be bought in the souvenir shop for a few dollars.

A few yards from Treaty House is the magnificent *Whare Runanga*, a Maori Meeting House, with the carvings and symbols of several Maori tribes from Northland. This is not at all typical as every tribe has its own meeting house known as a *marae*. *Waitangi Reserve on the Waitangi River estuary | daily 9am–5pm, 7pm in summer | 25 NZ$, valid on two consecutive days | www.waitangi.net.nz*

FOOD & DRINK

POCO LOCO
Spanish tapas. *Dinner daily | Marsden Rd. | tel. 09 4 02 83 88 | Budget*

INSIDER TIP WAIKOKOPU CAFÉ
Idyllically located in Waitangi Reserve. Breakfast and lunch served daily. *Tel. 09 4 02 62 75 | Budget–Moderate*

SHOPPING

THE CABBAGE TREE
Very tasteful souvenir shop where you can find lovely garments made of wool and cotton, wooden and jade souvenirs and gifts, and original prints made by New Zealand artits. The two shops are open daily: *Williams St.* and *Maritime Building | www.thecabbagetree.co.nz*

LEISURE & SPORTS

SEA-FISHING
The Bay is a paradise for sea-anglers who – between Dec and June – try their luck catching swordfish, for example, that can weigh up to 200kg. *Wild Bill | 40 Marsden Rd. | tel. 09 4 02 70 85 | www.wildbill.co.nz*

GOLF
Waitangi Golf Club has an 18-hole couse, idyllically situated on the Bay near Treaty House. All necessary equipment can be hired on the spot. *Tel. 09 4 02 77 13*

DIVING
One excursion takes you to the Greenpeace ship, the 'Rainbow Warrior', that was sunk by the French secret service in Auckland in 1985 and now lies as a marine memorial in the bay off *Cavalli Island* at a depth of 22m (72ft). The starting point for diving tours is either Paihia *(Paihia Dive | Williams Rd. | tel. 09 4 02 75 51 | www.divenz. com)* or Matauri Bay, with INSIDER TIP *Matauri Bay Holiday Park*, beautifully located on the beach *(campsite and chalets | tel. 09 4 05 05 25 | www.matauribay.co.nz | Budget–Moderate).*

WHERE TO STAY

BLUE PACIFIC QUALITY APARTMENTS
A lovely small apartment hotel with a 'million dollar view' of Paihia Beach. *12 rooms | 166 Marsden Rd. | tel. 09 4 02 73 94 | www.bluepacific.co.nz | Moderate*

SALTWATER LODGE
Centrally and quietly located, clean, with a view of the Bay. '5 star' accommodation for backpackers. *19 rooms | 14 Kings Rd. |*

tel. 09 4 02 70 75 | www.saltwaterlodge.co.nz | Budget

INFORMATION

BAY OF ISLANDS I-SITE
Marsden Rd. (Maritime Building) | tel. 09 4 02 73 45 | www.northland.org.nz

WHERE TO GO

FAR NORTH
(134 B1–2) (*🕮 F–G2*)
The northern tip of New Zealand's North Island is also called Far North District. Cynics refer to the region as 'the less North' – 'winter-less, job-less, road-less and penniless'. It's well worth booking a trip to Cape Reinga and ★ *Ninety Mile Beach* from Paihia or Kerikeri, which will take about 11 hours. The journey is long and the beach (which is actually only 96km (60mi) long – the name presumably comes from an error made eons ago) between Cape Reinga and Ahipara should not be driven on in a hire car, as your insurance will not cover the beach.
In the equally impressive scenery around *Cape Reinga*, where the Tasman Sea meets the Pacific, there is a post office, a pretty lighthouse and, right at the bottom of a cliff, a pohutukawa tree. It is here, or so the Maori believe, that their dead take leave of New Zealand to return to their homeland, the legendary Hawaiki. Excursions are organised by *Fullers Great Sights | Paihia | tel. 0800 65 33 39 | www.dolphincruises.co.nz*. Information under *www.fndc.govt.nz*

KAWAKAWA
(134 C3) (*🕮 H3*)
The original ● INSIDER TIP public WC building on the main shopping street, designed by Friedensreich Hundertwasser both inside and out, has livened up this

otherwise quiet spot 15km (9½mi) south of Paihia. The gallery and shop opposite, *The Grass Hut*, sells works by the famous artist.

KERIKERI
(134 C3) (*🕮 H3*)
Farmers sell kiwis, oranges and tomatoes on the roadside in the 'fruitbowl of Northland' some 25km (15½mi) north of Paihia. In the small harbour bay in Kerikeri (pop. 5500) is *Mission House*, built in 1822 and the *Stone Store*, the oldest stone building in New Zealand (1835). *Rewa's Village*, above the marina, is an open-air museum with a replica of a Maori village *(Kainga)* from the time before the arrival of the

The dead reputedly leave New Zealand from Cape Reinga for legendary Hawaiki

Europeans *(Sept–April daily 9am–5pm, otherwise 10am–4pm | 7 NZ$)*.

The sweet-toothed cannot help but make a beeline for the ● **INSIDER TIP** homemade chocolates in Makana Confections. Macadamia Popcorn *(daily 9am–5.30pm | Kerikeri Rd.)* is not to be missed. You can spend the night in the clean and spacious apartments in the *Ora Ora Resort*, quietly but centrally located near the marina *(28 Landing Rd. | tel. 09 4 07 35 98 | Expensive)*.

RUSSELL/BAY OF ISLANDS
(134–135 C–D3) *(ꕹ H3)*

Close to Russell (pop. 1500), now a sleepy little village on the Bay of Islands east of Paihia, is a place that was once the na-

tional capital of New Zealand. At this time Russel was still called Kororareka and became known as the 'Hell Hole of the Pacific' due to rough-shod whalers and loose morals. After the signing of the Treaty of Waitangi, New Zealand's first capital was established in Okiato, just a few miles away towards Opua. Okiato was swiftly renamed Russell after the Secretary of State for the Colonies. When Auckland became the capital, Okiato was virtually deserted and Kororareka became known as Russell instead.

Bullet holes from the turbulent past can still be seen in the walls of *Christ Church* in Russell which dates from 1835 *(Church St./Robertson Rd.)*.

You can't see the sky for the trees in Waipoua Kauri Forest

From ✺ *Flagstaff Hill* north of Russell, a lovely view across the Bay of Islands to Paihia can be enjoyed in the late afternoon before sampling the beer in *The Duke of Marlborough* on the waterfront. The pub was the first in New Zealand to be licenced to sell alcohol. The *Russell Museum* has a model of James Cook's ship 'Endeavour' *(daily 10am–4pm | York St. | 12 NZ$)*.

Fish specialities are served in historical surroundings in *The Gables (The Strand | tel. 09 4 03 76 18 | Moderate–Expensive)*. The ✺ **INSIDER TIP** *Omata Estate* is a small wine-producing estate with a restaurant, from which you can enjoy a wonderful view over the Bay. Superb lunches! *(Aucks Rd. | just beyond the ferry terminal in Opua towards Russell | tel. 09 4 03 80 07 | www.omata.co.nz | Moderate–Expensive)*. Inexpensive cabins can be rented at *Russell Top Ten Holiday Park (Longbeach Rd. | tel. 09 4 03 78 26 |*

Budget), or book a room ✺ with a view of the Bay in *Te Maiki Villas (9 rooms | Flagstaff Rd. | tel. 09 4 03 70 46 | Expensive)*. ✺ Cruises around the Bay in a stylish tall ship, accompanied by delphins, are offered by *R. Tucker Thompson (10am from Russell | 140 NZ$ | tel. 09 4 02 84 30 | www.tucker. co.nz)*.

Information: *Bay of Islands Maritime and Historic Park Headquarters | The Strand (next to Russell Museum) | daily 8.30am– 5pm | tel. 09 4 03 90 05 | www.doc.govt. nz or www.russellnz.com*. The audiovisual show on the flora and fauna in Northland is well-worth watching.

WAIMATE NORTH MISSION HOUSE
(134 C3) (ØØ G3)

This, the first inland mission station, was built by Samuel Marsden, the so-called 'apostle of New Zealand', 21km (13mi) west of Paihia in 1831. *Oct–March Sat–Wed 10am–5pm*

WAIPOUA KAURI FOREST
(134 C3) (*ω G3*)

Tane Mahuta, 'Lord of the Forest' (51m/167ft high, 14m/46ft circumference) and *Te Matua Ngahere,* 'Father of the Forest' (30m/98ft), the highest kauri trees in New Zealand, are on Hwy 12 between Omapere and Dargaville. The extensive and impressive *Kauri Museum (daily 9am–5pm | www.kauri-museum.com)* highlights the history of the protected kauri trees that were once the victim of unscrupulous felling by early settlers for their valuable hardwood. 'Gum diggers' traded with the resin that was used as an adhesive, tapped from wounds slashed into the wooden giants. Information centre at the southern end of the park *(Nov–March Mon–Fri 8am–4.30pm, Sat/Sun 9am–4pm). 70km (44mi) southwest*

ROTORUA

(137 D4) (*ω K6*) **All roads lead to Rotorua. The town, located virtually in the middle of North Island, is a tourist honeypot being the cultural and artistic centre of the Maori as well as a steaming ● geothermal region rich in forests and lakes.**

The volcanic faultline from Mt. Ruapehu (Tongariro National Park) to volcanic White Island is 150km (93mi) long. Despite the streams of tourists, the 68,000 residents still live largely from forestry and the wood processing industry.

SIGHTSEEING

AGRODOME LEISURE PARK
Tourist spectacle centred around the 19 breeds of New Zealand sheep presented in a 1-hour show *(daily 9.30am, 11am, 2.30pm | 24 NZ$ | Ngongotaha | Riverdale Park | www.agrodome.co.nz).*

Right next door you can go 'zorbing' – rolling down a track in a huge, inflatable transparent sphere or racing around a tight circuit in jet boats.

KIWI ENCOUNTER ●
The numbers of the shaggy, nocturnal and almost blind flightless bird are given a helping hand at this nature conservancy in *Rainbow Springs (www.rainbowsprings.co.nz)* nature park. The 45-minute guided tour takes you through the hatching and rearing sections – perhaps a chick will hatch in front of your eyes. *Daily 10am–4pm | Fairy Springs Rd. | www.kiwiencounter.co.nz*

OHINEMUTU
A long time ago, the first Maori settled here among the geothermal vents in what is now a suburb of Rotorua. Old carvings can be admired in the meeting house.

ROTORUA MUSEUM
Carefully restored former baths built in 1907 in the Tudor style. The permanent collection displays cultural artefacts from the local Rotorua region Te Arawa Maori tribe. In front of the building is a cricket pitch and a bowling lawn. Impressive video of the 1886 eruption of Tarawara. *In summer daily 9.30am–8pm, pool daily 9am–5pm | 13 NZ$ | Government Gardens | tel. 07 3 49 43 50*

SKYLINE SKYRIDES ☙
Hill with a lovely view of Lake Rotorua, variety of outdoor activities (such as a concrete track luge run) and a restaurant. *Fairy Springs Rd., near Kiwi Encounter*

WHAKAREWAREWA/TE PUIA
Also known as 'Whaka' – a geothermal area in Rotorua with mud pools and geysers such as *Pohutu,* which attracts the most attention with its fountains of up to 30m (100ft).

The *New Zealand Maori Arts and Crafts Institute*, with a good assortment of souvenirs in the shop, is in Whaka. The carvers' workshop is well worth a visit. The design of the building on the *marae* (Maori meeting place) symbolises the human figure or ancestor present through the shape of the building. The long ridge beam forms the backbone, the struts to both sides represent the ribs. At the front, kingposts frame the doorway like two mighty arms. *Hemo Rd. | daily 8.30am–5pm | folk concerts daily 10.15am, 12.15pm and 3.15pm | entrance fee for geothermal area and concert incl. guided tour 55 NZ$*

★ ● *Hangi* is the name of food cooked in a traditional earth oven that consists largely of sweet potatoes, mussels and wild boar. The best food is served at the Mai-Ora performance in Whakarewarewa *(Te Puia)*. The show on the *marea* is good. Combine a tour (2 hours) through the geothermal reserve before the *hangi* (6.15pm). *Tour and hangi 145 NZ$. Information: www.tepuia.co.nz.* Authentic performances on a *marae* are also organised by *Tamaki Tours (105 NZ$ | tel. 07 3 46 28 23)*. Pick-up bus service operated.

FOOD & DRINK

Most restaurants are on Tutanekai Street ('The Street'). Those who fancy a *hangi* have to make do with the large tourist events in the hotels.

CAPERS

Modern-style café. Delicious lunches and delicatessen. Breakfast until noon. *Lunch/dinner | 1181 Eruera St. | tel. 07 3 48 88 18 | Budget–Moderate*

SHOPPING

Richly decorated carvings have always been a characteristic of the Polynesians. Nowhere else is the selection of Maori art (both industrial and handmade) as great as in the souvenir shops in Rotorua.

LEISURE & SPORTS

AIR SAFARIS ⛷

Flights over the Rotorua geothermal reserve: *Volcanic Air Safaris (city lakefront | tel. 07 3 48 99 84)* are good value for money. Excursions to the crater of the still active Mt. Tarawera are especially memorable: a four-wheel drive bus takes you to the crater, followed by a 1-hour hike and a 15-minute return flight by helicopter *(duration approx. 4 hours from/to Whakarewarewa/Te Puia | 475 NZ$ | tel. 07 3 48 12 23 | www.helipro.co.nz)*.

SWIMMING

The *Polynesian Spa* right on Lake Rotorua, has more than 30 different pools and 26 separate private pools, fed by various mineral water springs. A visit on a clear evening is especially lovely. *Hinemoa St. next to the Bath House and Museum | daily 6.30am–11pm | 25–45 NZ$ | www.polynesianspa.co.nz*

WHERE TO STAY

Fenton Street is where the hotels are. Special deals are clearly advertised.

HOTEL GEYSERLAND ⛷

Rooms with a view of the mud pools are the best. Just ask! *66 rooms | 424 Fenton St. | tel. 07 3 48 20 39 | www.silveroaks.co.nz | Moderate*

WAITETI LAKEFRONT MOTEL

Unpretentious accommodation away from Rotorua directly on the lake, with boats for hire. *8 rooms | Ngongotaha | 7 Arnold St. | tel. 07 3 57 42 94 | www.jackanddis.co.nz | Moderate*

Traditional Maori carving: the best selection anywhere is in Rotorua

INFORMATION

VISITOR INFORMATION
1167 Fenton St. | tel. 07 3 48 51 79 | www. rotoruanz.com. Helpful map with main sights in and around the town *(1 NZ$).*

WHERE TO GO

BURIED VILLAGE
(137 D4) *(ω K6)*
The villiage buried after Tarawera erupted in 1886 is now an open-air museum. The drive past the Green and Blue Lakes provides romantic views of the volcano and lake. *Daily 9am–5pm | Tarawera Rd. (16km/10mi from Rotorua) | 15 NZ$*

LAKE TAUPO
(136 C4–5) *(ω J–K7)*
Covering 255mi² New Zealand's largest lake is in the crater of an extinct volcano and is famous for its enormous stocks of trout. Good restaurants, e.g. *Villino (45* *Horomatangi St. | tel. 07 3 77 44 78)* and motels, e.g. *Clearwater, Karaka Tree* and *de Brett's,* with a campsite and hot pools, make a stay in the little town of *Taupo* very pleasant. An excursion with the sailing ship 'Barbary' across the lake (Maori rock carvings), bungee jumping and a trip through Wairakei Park with a visit to a prawn farm *(guided tours daily from 9am | 320g of freshwater crayfish cost approx. 32NZ$)* and *Honey Hive (daily 9am–5pm),* are also interesting. The *Huka Falls* are in a narrow gorge through which the Waikato River races (at 400km/250mi, New Zealand's longest river). Jet boats leave from the prawn farm. Information: *Visitor Information Taupo | Hwy 5 | Main St. | tel. 07 3 76 00 27 | www.laketauponz.com. 75km (46½mi) southwest*

HAMILTON
(136 B3) *(ω J6)*
The country's largest inland city (pop. 141,000) is at the centre of things but is

not really an urban metropolis. Nevertheless, Hamilton is worth visiting simply for the extremely good *Waikato Museum (daily 10am–4.30pm | 1 Grantham St.),* where Maori history is presented in a fascinating way as is the natural history of the region. Right next door, the old post office is now *Arts Post (daily 10am–4.30pm | 120 Victoria St. | www.artspost. co.nz),* a shop jam-packed with art and crafts – a real treasure-trove for souvenir hunters.

at *Palate (Tue–Sat dinner | 170 Victoria St. | tel. 07 8 34 29 21 | Moderate).*

Richard O'Brien spent his youth in Hamilton before going to London aged 22. He later wrote *The Rocky Horror Show* (first performed in 1973) in which he played the butler Riff Raff. A statue of him and a webcam are on Victoria St. (level with no. 230). The ideal spot for phoning home on your mobile *(www.riffraffstatue.org).*

New Zealand's surfing mecca is only some 50km (30mi) from Hamilton: *Raglan (www.*

The Renaissance area in Hamilton Gardens: perfect for a gentle stroll

A breath of fresh air can be enjoyed in *Hamilton Gardens* which cover an area of 124 acres to the southeast of the city and along the Waikato River. *Victoria St.* (between Garden Place and Hood St.) is the place to head to for a bite to eat and a drink. This is where students at the renowned university meet up in the evenings. The omnipresent Thai, Chinese and Indian restaurants are good and cheap. If you prefer quality Kiwi cuisine, book a table

raglan.net.nz) is a small but lively village on the west coast. The waves in *Manu Bay* and *Whale Bay* are perfect for passionate surfers. Beginners will be well looked after at *Raglan Surf School* that also has equipment for hire and simple accommodation near the beach *(5b Whaanga Rd. | Whale Bay | tel. 07 8 25 78 73 | www. raglansurfingschool.co.nz).* Courses in the *Old School Arts Centre (www.raglanarts centre.co.nz)* in traditional Maori crafts

such as carving and weaving are extremely popular – and not just when the weather is bad. The 😊 *Raglan Creative Market (9am–2pm)* is held outdoors every second Sunday in the month and sells all sorts of organic home-grown produce.
Information: *Waikato i-SITE | Hamilton | corner Cavo/Angelsea St. | tel. 07 8 39 33 60 | www.hamiltonwaikato.com*

NGARUAWAHIA
(136 B3) (*⌀ J6*)
It was here in 1858 that the majority of tribes in so-called King Country recognised Potatau I as the first Maori king. Queen Te Atairangikaahu, a descendant of his, carried out her representative duties – having little political power – in the *Turangawaewae marae* until her death in 2006. She endured the same fate as woman in many tribes, as she was not allowed to hold a speech in the grounds of a *marae*. Her eldest son, Tuheitia Paki, is her successor. The 'kingdom' can be seen from the outside (from the river bridge on the SH 1) but is not open to the public. In mid May, a regatta is held here with huge war canoes *(waka taua)*. *110km (68mi) northwest*

TAURANGA
(136–137 C–D3) (*⌀ K6*)
Definitely the most beautiful part of Tauranga (pop. 120,000) starts at the neighbouring resort *Mt. Maunganui*, named after the 230m (755ft)-high hill on the sea. A fine sandy beach stretches as far as the eye can see – actually 15km (9½mi) long – to beyond Papamoa. There is a lively relaxed atmosphere along the water and sufers with boards under their arms congregate on the promenade. The choice of accommodation is correspondingly wide. Some of the rooms in the *Ocean Waves Motel (16 rooms | 74 Marine Parade | tel. 07 5 75 45 94 or 0800 74*

30 19 | *Moderate)* have a view of the sea. *Beachside Holiday Park (1 Adama Ave. | tel. 07/5 75 44 71 | Budget)* for motorhomes is central and close to the beach, and the *hot saltwater pools (Mon–Sat 6am–10pm, Sun 8am–10pm | 9 Adams Ave.)* are right next door.
The arched harbour bridge across the sheltered bay leads to Tauranga's lively city centre. Restaurants, cafés and bars are clustered around the water down the coastal road The Strand. The locals tend to go a little bit further to the small fishing port where the *Fresh Fish Market (lunch/dinner daily | 1 Dive Crescent)* not only sells the day's catch but also crisp fish and chips. *90km (56mi) to the north.*
Information: *i-SITE | 95 Willow St. | tel. 07 5 78 81 03 | www.gotauranga.co.nz*

TE PUKE
(137 D3) (*⌀ K6*)
This tiny place calls itself the 'Kiwifruit Capital of the World' and turns into a hive of activity every year in May and June when the kiwis in the sunny *Bay of Plenty* are harvested. *Kiwifruit Country* displays (and sells) everything that has to do with the 'Chinese gooseberry' *(guided tours of the kiwi plantations on Hwy 2 daily 9am–3.45pm). 50km (31mi) north*

VOLCANIC REGION
(137 D3–4) (*⌀ K6–7*)
Walks through *Hell's Gate (on Hwy 30 towards Whakatane)* which take just over an hour, are perhaps more interesting than the Whaka geothermal reserve in Rotorua. The seemingly unreal ★ *Waimangu Volcanic Valley*, 23km (14½mi) south of Rotorua, with its natural bubbling water, is especially worth seeing and boasts having 'the world's largest hot-water spring'. The attractions at the *Waiotapu Thermal Wonderland*, 30km (19mi) to the south, are the colourful champagne pools *(both*

No drinking: the Champagne Pool im Waiotapu Thermal Wonderland

geothermal sites are on Hwy 5 between Rotorua and Taupo). You can give Lady Knox Geyser a miss: it is coaxed to perform at 10.15am by adding soap powder and is not particularly exciting.

WAIRAKEI TERRACES (136 C4) (*∅ K7*)
Beautiful circular hiking trail (45 mins.) on the edge of *Thermal Valley* where geothermal sources are used to generate electricity. The (artificially created) silica terraces and explanations on the Maori culture are highlights. *Daily 9am–5pm | on SH, 1½ min. drive to the north of Taupo | 22 NZ$ | www.wairakeiterraces.co.nz*

WAITOMO (GLOWWORM CAVES) ●
(136 B4) (*∅ J7*)
The caves with their millions of glowworms are a magnet for day-trippers *(daily 9am–5pm | 46 NZ$ | www.waitomo.com)*. The **INSIDER TIP** *Lost World Tandem Absail (tel. 07 8 78 77 88 | 300 NZ$ for 4 hours | www. waitomo.co.nz)* is quite an adventure: absail 100m (328ft) down into the limestone cave where fossils of oysters the size of plates and underground waterfalls await you. For the everso-slightly-less courageous, try *blackwater rafting (Black Labyrinth)* on an inflatable inner tube through a dark cave *(Legendary Blackwater Rafting | daily 9am–4pm | 3 hours | 120 NZ$ | tel. 07 8 78 62 19 | www.waitomo.com)*.

For those not so keen on being underground, spend some time at *Woodlyn Park* and its fun *Farm Show*. And why not stay the night in an unusual place – such as in a plane, railway carriage, ship or Hobbit cave? *(10 rooms | 1177 Waitomo Valley Rd. | tel. 07 8 78 88 66 | www.woodlynpark.*

Ohope Beach to the east is the most popular. Barely 50km (31mi) offshore, pillars of smoke billow up above *White Island*, an active volcanic site which can only be accessed on a guided excursion – either by air *(Vulcan Helicopters | from Whakatane Airport | duration 2½ hours | tel. 07 3 08 41 88 or 0800 80 43 54 | www.vulcanheli.co.nz)* or by boat *(White Island Tours Pee Jay | 15 The Strand East | duration 6 hours | tel. 07 3 08 03 03 | www.whiteisland.co.nz)*. Whale and delphin-watching boat trips are also available on the open sea. On some you can swim with the dolphins. *(e.g. Whale & Dolphin Watch | 96 The Strand | tel. 07 3 08 20 01 or 0800 3 54 77 37 | www.whalesanddolphinwatch.co.nz)*. 85km (53mi) east

WANGANUI

(139 D2) *(⫘ J9)* **The Whanganui River was once known as 'The Rhine of Maoriland' and was a popular river for cruises at the beginning of the 20th century.**
A little bit of yesteryear can still be experienced if you journey up the river between Wanganui and Pipiriki on the ● INSIDER TIP restored steamship 'Waimarie' *(Whanganui River Cruises | daily 2pm | 2 hours | 33 NZ$ | www.riverboat.co.nz)* or by car. Wanganui (pop. 40,000) on the flood plains is a sleepy place and even more so in the evenings. *Putiki Church* has some interesting Maori carvings *(2 Anaua St. | in Putiki)*.

co.nz | Budget–Expensive). Alternatively, you can be more conventional and choose a confortable room in the good, centrally located and popular *Top Ten Holiday Park (12 Waitomo Caves Rd. | tel. 07 8 78 76 39 or 0508 49 86 60 | www.waitomopark.co.nz | Budget)*. Information: *i-SITE/Waitomo Caves Discovery Center* with interesting displays on the geology of the karst rock caves *(21 Waitomo Caves Rd. in the centre | tel. 07 8 78 76 40 | www.waitomocaves.com)*. Despite the number of major tourist attractions there is neither a petrol station nor a groceries in the village. *160km (100mi) west*

WHAKATANE
(137 D3) *(⫘ L6)*
This small coastal town *(www.whakatane.com)* is surrounded by wonderful beaches.

WHANGANUI REGIONAL MUSEUM
Contains one of the largest and most beautiful jade and greenstone collections in the world, as well as crafts and a Maori war canoe. *Mon–Sat 10am–4.30pm, Sun 1pm–4.30pm | 4 NZ$ | Watt St./Civic Centre*

WANGANUI

LEISURE & SPORTS

WHANGANUI RIVER

The river is some 315km (196mi) long. From its source on the west flank of Mt. Tongariro, it flows some distance through *Whanganui National Park*, to which it gave its name. From Taumarunui it can easily be navigated by canoe or kajak as far as Wanganui. The 234km (145mi) stretch passes through idyllic, jungle-like vegetation and over 240 easy rapids *(reservations e.g. Wades Landing Outdoors | Owhango | tel. 06 8 95 59 95 | www.whanganui.co.nz)*. The tranquility is sometimes disturbed by loud jetboats most of which set off from *Pipiriki*. The restored Colonial House in *Pipiriki*, built by Europeans at the end of the 19th century, houses an *information centre (daily 9am–5.30pm, only in summer)*. The road from Pipiriki to Wanganui is mostly surfaced but very twisty (and in some places extremely narrow for campervans). It follows the river for some 80km (50mi) past the few remaining Maori settlements. Join Al Muller on his INSIDER TIP mail run from Wanganui to Pipiriki (70 NZ$) and

Explore the virgin jungle in Whanganui National Park in complete safety

help him deliver the post on his 6-hour round. Nobody knows the area bettter than him! *Mon–Fri from 7.30am (max. 12 people) | tel. 06 3 45 34 75 | www.whanganuitours.co.nz*

INFORMATION

WANGANUI I-SITE

Also arranges accommodation. *31 Taupo Quay | tel. 06 3 49 05 08 | www.wanganui.com*

WELLINGTON

PALMERSTON NORTH (139 E3) (*❪❪ J9*)
Major centre (pop. 68,000) for the agri-culturally important district of *Manawatu* with a small rugby museum (*Mon–Sat 10am–4pm, Sun 1.30pm–4pm | 8 NZ$ | 87 Cuba St.*). 70km (43½mi) to the southeast.

TONGARIRO NATIONAL PARK
(139 D–E 1–2) (*❪❪ J8*)
New Zealand's oldest national park was a present from the Maori chieftain Te Heuheu to the British Crown in 1887 to protect this unique highland region. Ngauruhoe has erupted 60 times over the past 150 years. In 1953, Mt. Ruapehu erupted on Christmas Eve, killing 151. The eruptions in 1995 and 1996 were natural spectacles set against a snowy background and passed without incidence.

Volcanoes towering up to 2796m (9173ft) form an impressive setting for one of the most popular ski areas, the centre of which is above ❄ *Bayview Chateau Tongariro (64 rooms | tel. 07 8 92 38 09 | www. chateau.co.nz | Moderate–Expensive*) in Whakapapa, a luxury hotel built in 1929 in the style of an English mansion. The chair lift also runs in summer when you can take a day's hike to the rim of the crater (guided tours also available; *reservations: tel. 06 8 92 37 38 | approx. 60 NZ$ | 9.30am from base of Whakapapa lift*). Wonderful hikes such as the strenuous day's excursion **INSIDERTIP** 'Tongariro Crossing' (*excellent guided tour with Terry Blumhardt | www. walkingplaces.co.nz*) start from the hotel and *Whakapapa Village* – with campsite (*tel. 07 8 92 38 97 | www.whakapapa.net. nz*) and ranger station with displays on the flora and mountain scenery in the park (*daily 8am–5pm | entrance free*). Shops and good, cheap accommodation available in *National Park Village (at the crossroads of Hwy 4 and 47*). 290km (180mi) notheast

⚅ MAP INSIDE BACK COVER
(139 D5) (*❪❪ H10*) **Known as 'Windy Wellington', a bitter wind blows almost every day between the high-rises in the centre and across the hills with their pretty wooden detached houses.**

From the ❄ **INSIDERTIP** viewing plat-form on Mt. Victoria, 196m (643ft), you have a lovely view over the city and Port Nicholson as far as Petone. It was here that Wellington was founded in 1839 and, just one year later, the carpenter Samuel Parnell campaigned for the 8-hour work-ing day. *Cook Strait*, 23km (14¼mi) wide, separates North and South Islands. Wellington's main street, *Lambton Quay*, which was part of the foreshore before land reclamation and uplift caused by an earthquake in 1855, is always busy but even in the government district things never get that hectic.

> 🏙 **WHERE TO START?**
> **Lambton Quay:** The main shopping area stretches from Civic Square (visitor centre) to the gov-ernment district past the cable car (Botanic Gardens) and on towards the harbour promenade and the National Museum. The pedestri-anised Cuba Mall and the restau-rants and cafés on Courtney Place are nearby. The centre can easily be explored on foot. Parking is best on the harbour promenade.

For information on public transport see: *www.metlink.org.nz.* A hop-on-hop-off bus connects the most important sights *(daily 9.30am–4.30pm | leaving from the i-SITE | day pass 30 NZ$).*

BEEHIVE/PARLIAMENT HOUSE/ GOVERNMENT BUILDING

The round building that really does look like a beehive houses the ministries. The 70m (230ft)-high tower is connected to Parliament House. The public is allowed to listen to the heated discussions in the Debating Chamber (based on Westminster). 120 MPs govern over New Zealand, of which 7 are Maori representatives. Government Building (1876) is opposite. It is the second highest wooden building in the world – even if it does look as if it were made of stone. Free guided tours are held every day on the hour *Mon–Fri 10am–4pm, Sat 10am–3pm, Sun 11am–3pm (Parliament House and Library) | bookings: tel. 04 4 71 95 03 | www.parliament. nz | Government Building | Mon–Fri 9am–4.30pm, Sat/Sun 10am–3pm*

BOTANIC GARDENS

The Botanic Gardens with their areas of native forest and exotic plants form the highlight of a circular, 90-min. tour that starts at the ⭐ *cable car (280 Lambton Quay).* The funicular railway takes you up 122m (400ft) to the suburb of Kelburn. From there, a path leads through the 55-acre Botanic Gardens to *Lady Norwood Rose Garden* with some 2000 different types of rose *(in bloom from Nov–April)* and back to the city centre via *Bolton Street Memorial Park* with the graves of influential Wellingtonians.

KATHERINE MANSFIELD HOUSE

The birthplace of the authoress (1888–1923) famous for her short stories. Katherine Mansfield lived in this plain but carefully restored house for five years. *Tue–Sun 10am–4pm | 6 NZ$ | 25 Tinakori Rd.*

MUSEUM OF WELLINGTON CITY & SEA

Interesting displays on the history of the seafaring city. *Daily 10am–5pm | 8 NZ$ | The Bond Store | Queens Wharf | www. museumofwellington.co.nz*

THE NATIONAL TATTOO MUSEUM

An in-depth look into the world of the tattoo – or *moko* in Maori – which is very important to the Polynesians. *Daily noon–5.30pm | 87 Vivian St. | www.mokomuseum. org.nz*

TE PAPA (MUSEUM OF NEW ZEALAND) ⭐ ●

The focus of this ultramodern showpiece is on exhibitions on nature, Polynesian history and the settlement of the country. Admission is free but a charge is made to use the high-tech simulators. The INSIDER TIP▶ souvenir shop is worth a visit for its art cards and lovely jewellery. *Fri–Wed 10am–6pm, Thu 10am–9pm | Cable St. | www.tepapa.govt.nz*

WETA CAVES

A fascinating look at the secrets of film animation. *Weta* is the trick studio made world-famous by the New Zealand director Peter Jackson *(Lord of the Rings)* and the recipient of several Oscars (e.g. for *Avator*). Masses of original souvenirs to get your hands on and an impressive 20-minute film, but no studio tours. *Daily 9am–5.30pm | Cnr Camperdown Rd./ Weka St. | in Miramar | www.wetanz.co.nz* For tours to various filmsets around the capital (incl. *Lord of the Rings*) see *www. mo vietours.co.nz.*

ZEALANDIA/KARORI SANCTUARY

An extensive park on the western edge of Wellington with rare birds and wild tuatara – a lizard-like reptile. 30km (18½mi) of paths criss-cross the site. Guided tours also available *(daily 9am–*

If you take the funicular to the top, you will have a lovely view of Wellington

5pm | 55 NZ$ | Waiapu Rd. | www.visitzea landia.com). An unusual natural experience is to take the *Night Tour*. Only endemic plants line the well-tended paths through the wild and romantic *Otari-Wiltons Bush Reserve (free admission | 160 Wilton Rd. | www.wellingtonnz.com)*.

FOOD & DRINK

Wellington has excellent restaurants. Sometimes prices are higher than elsewhere. Places to head for include: Courtenay Place *(e.g. Monsoon Poon | 12 Blair St. | tel. 04 8 03 35 55 | Moderate)*, ⚓ Queens Wharf or Customhouse Quay with lovely sea views (restaurants *Wagamama Moderate–Expensive, Portofino Moderate–Expensive* and the trendy coffeehouse *Mojo | 33 Customhouse Quay | www. mojocoffee.co.nz*, as well as *Shed 5 | tel. 04 4 99 90 69 | Moderate–Expensive)* and Upper Cuba St. *(Logan Brown Moderate–*

Expensive, Caffe Italiano and *Seamarket | tel. 04 3848461 | opposite Quality Hotel | Budget).* 🕒 *Commonsense Organics (260 Wakefield St.)* and *Moore Wilson's Fresh Market (corner Tory St./College St.)* are of interest to health-conscious self-catering holidaymakers.

INSIDER TIP ERNESTO

Vegetarian and delicious – and the coffee is simply superb. Open until late at night *(breakfast, lunch, dinner daily | 178 Cuba St. | tel. 04 3 84 70 14 | Budget–Moderate)*. Diagonally opposite (no. 161) is *Floriditas (Budget)*, a good alternative.

MATTERHORN

Sometimes super, sometimes just about okay, but always imaginatively prepared and presented. As a result, it is always full. Reservation advisable. *Lunch, dinner daily | Cuba St. | tel. 04 3 84 33 59 | Moderate– Expensive*

Sitting, standing, lying? Unusual sculptures in Kura Gallery

SHOPPING

Unusual jewellery and carved objects can be found at *Iwi Art (19 Tory St.)*, at *Ora (23 Allen St.)* and next door in *Kura Gallery* as well as at *Iko Iko (118 Cuba Mall)*.

LEISURE & SPORTS

SWIMMING

The beaches frequented by the Wellingtonians are along *Oriental Parade* (near the city centre and the new cruise liner terminal), in *Island Bay* and *Lyall Bay* (with a view towards South Island), *Days Bay* in Muritai and in up-market *Eastbourne (can also be reached by ferry: www.eastbywest.co.nz)*. Sometimes the quality of the water is poor.

ENTERTAINMENT

The bars *The Coyote* and *The Grand* on Courtenay Place, for example, can be rec-ommended. After 10pm many pubs turn into discos. For events see *www.wotzon.com*

WHERE TO STAY

Although you pay extra for being in the capital, there are some good weekend offers especially in top-category hotels.

QUALITY HOTEL/COMFORT HOTEL

Two hotels in one complex. The Comfort Hotel is slightly cheaper. Ideal location for townies. *180 rooms altogether | 223 Cuba St. | tel. 04 385 2156 | Moderate–Expensive (Quality) | tel. 04 385 2153 | Moderate (Comfort) | www.qualitywellington.com*

THE WELLESLEY BOUTIQUE HOTEL

Once a club for the hotel branch, it is now a charming hotel with wood panelling and elegant furnishings. Central location. *13 rooms | 2–8 Maginnity St. | tel.*

04 4 74 13 08 | www.thewellesley.co.nz | *Expensive*

WELLINGTON WATERFRONT MOTORHOME PARK

You won't find anything more central than this! This motorhome overnight park on the harbour has sanitary facilities and is close to the ferries to South Island and just a hop, skip and jump to the centre. Perfect for a walking touring of the city. *(Waterloo Quay | tel. 04 3 84 45 11 | approx. 50 NZ$ for 2 people | www.wwmp.co.nz).*

FERRIES

Interislander ferries run 3 times a day between North and South Islands. The journey takes a good 3 hours *(from Aotea Quay, 2 km/1¼mi from the centre | tel. 0800 80 28 02 | tel. 04 4 98 33 02 | www. interislander.co.nz).* Advance reservation essential at weekends and peak periods. Stand-by rates are not cheaper. Alternatively, the *Bluebridge* ferry leaves from the terminal opposite the main railway station in Wellington *(4 times daily | tel. 0800 84 48 44 or tel. 04 4 71 61 88 | www. bluebridge.co.nz).*

INFORMATION

WELLINGTON I-SITE
101 Wakefield St. Civic Square | tel. 04 8 02 48 60 | www.wellingtonnz.com

WHERE TO GO

KAPITI COAST
(139 D4) (ⓜ H–J10)

The stretch of coast to the north lined with beaches is the Wellingtonians' favourite recreational area. It is named after the off-shore island Kapiti – a nature reserve that is home to many species of bird threatened by extinction. Access only with a permit issued by the DOC in Wellington *(tel. 04 3 84 77 70 | www.doc.govt.nz).* Due to considerable demand, reservation at least 1–2 months in advance is advisable. The boat transfer from Paraparaumu has to be booked separately *(Kapiti Marine Charter | tel. 04 2 97 25 85 or 0800 43 37 79).* Natural history tours and simple accommodation are provided by local Maori *(Kapiti Island Alive | tel. 06 3 62 66 06 | www.kapitiislandalive.co.nz).*

Car fanatics will find it difficult to tear themselves away from Paraparaumu. *Southward Car Museum (daily 9am–5pm | 10 NZ$ | on SH1 | Otaihanga Rd.)* has some 200 fantastic oldtimers, including Marlene Dietrich's soft top Cadillac. *50km (31mi) north*

MARTINBOROUGH/WAIRARAPA
(139 D5) (ⓜ J10)

This delightful village, 80km (50mi) to the east, is the centre of the Wairarapa wine region that produces the best but also the most expensive wines in the country *(e.g. Ata Rangi | www.atarangi. co.nz or Schubert Wines | www.schubert. co.nz).* Guided *wine tours* from Wellington are popular *(Dynamic Tours | tel. 04 4 78 85 33 | www.dynamictours.co.nz).* Martinborough Wine Centre *(daily 10am–5pm | 6 Kitchener St. | tel. 06 3 06 90 40 | www. martinboroughwinecentre.co.nz)* not only stocks many local wines but also rents out bikes *(35 NZ$/day)* for tours through the vineyards and to wine-growers.

Right next to the public swimming pool is a basic but quietly situated campsite. Cabins also available *(Martinborough Village Camping, corner Princess/Dublin St. | tel. 06 3 06 89 46 | Budget).* *Est Bar and Eatery* in the old post office *(Wed–Sun dinner, Sat/Sun also lunch | 8 The Square | tel. 06 3 06 96 65 | Moderate)* can be recommended. Information: *www.wairarapa nz.com*

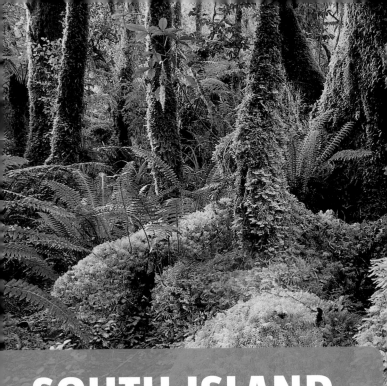

SOUTH ISLAND

The New Zealand tourist industry energetically promotes South Island's uniqueness. There is (almost) everything here: impressive mountains with snow-capped peaks and glaciers, wonderful trails through lush vegetation, barren upland plateaus inhabited by sheep, crystal-clear lakes and beaches which make even South Sea Islanders turn green with envy.

Nobody will resent it if you spend a little more time on South rather than North Island. After all, South Island, covering 58,200mi² is about 20% bigger than North Island. And there are any number of scenic places that you often have to yourself.

AORAKI MT. COOK

(143 E1) (*ω D13*) The Maori call it Aoraki (or Aorangi) – 'the mountain that pierces the clouds'. More recent maps mark it both as Mt. Cook and Aoraki.

It is still New Zealand's highest mountain although it lost an incredible 14 million cubic metres of rock and glacial ice in December 1991 when 10m broke off the peak. Its exact height is now 3754m (12,316ft). But since Aoraki hides its peak in thick clouds 240 days a year, its 'new'

Gardens, glaciers, mountains: Nature, the imaginative landscape gardener, has really pulled out all the stops on South Island

summit is not really going to be noticed. Whether the 55km (34mi) trip down the well-built State Highway (SH) 80 to Mount Cook Village is worth its while, depends first and foremost on the weather *(information tel. 03 435 11 86)*.

Apart from its location fronting the mountain range, the little village of Mount Cook only has a few isolated and generally expensive places to stay. There is a campsite as an alternative, but few eateries.

LEISURE & SPORTS

GRAND TRAVERSE ⚡

★ Flights around the mountain start from Lake Tekapo, Franz Josef and Fox Glacier. *(Air Safaris | approx. 310 NZ$ | tel. 03 6 80 68 80 | www.airsafaris.co.nz)*

AORAKI MT. COOK

The stuff of dreams: Lake Tekapo at an altitude of 710 metres (2,300ft)

WHERE TO STAY

THE HERMITAGE HOTEL
This renovated luxury hotel with its ☆ panoramic restaurant are at the foot of Mt. Cook. *104 rooms | tel. 03 4 35 18 09 | www.mount-cook.com | Expensive*

MOUNT COOK YOUTH HOSTEL
The only cheap accommodation. *70 rooms | NP, Bowen/Kitchener Dr. | tel. 03 4 35 18 20 | www.yha.co.nz | Budget*

INFORMATION

AORAKI MT. COOK NATIONAL PARK VISITOR CENTRE
Tel. 03 4 35 11 86 | www.mtcook.org.nz

WHERE TO GO

LAKE TEKAPO ☆ (143 E1) (*ш D13–14*)
Like a landscape painting: the small *Church of the Good Shepherd*, made of rough-hewn stone, sits on the turquoise Lake Tekapo with snow-covered mountains in the background. The lake, at an altitude of 710m (2330ft), owes its unique colour to the extremely fine powdered stone washed into the cold water by glacial mountain streams. Lake Tekapo in partly in Mackenzie Country, an area of undulating hills that are perfect for cross-country skiing and hiking. The region wants to become the first Unesco *World Heritage Site* for its starry night sky, as there is no light pollution from built-up areas to dis-

turb this nocturnal spectacle. The *observatory* on Mt. John is well worth visiting *(signposted from the SH 8 | tour daily 10am–4pm | approx. 40 min. | 20 NZ$; stargazing tour daily from 8.30pm | approx. 2 hours | 85 NZ$ | tel. 03 6 80 69 60 | www.earthandsky.co.nz, www.starlightreserve.org).* The Chalet *(6 flats | tel. 03 6 80 67 74 | www.thechalet.co.nz | Moderate–Expensive)*, run by a Swiss couple, is a lovely place to stay in Lake Tekapo. ☆☆ *Scenic Resort* on the SH 8 *(18 rooms | tel. 03 6 80 68 08 | www.laketekapo.com | Moderate)* overlooks the lake. You can camp right on the shore at *Lake Tekapo Holiday Park (cabins and rooms also available | Lakeside Dr. | tel. 03 6 80 68 25 or 0800 85 38 53 | Budget).* 125km (68mi) to the south. Information: *www.laketekapountouched.co.nz*

TASMAN GLACIER ☆☆ **(143 E1)** *(🔖 D13)*
This impressive glacier is 29km (18mi) long and up to 2km (1¼mi) wide. Helicopter companies enable people to ski down the 13km (8mi) stretch. By car, the snout of the glacier can be reached from Mount Cook Village heading for Blue Lake *(approx. 8km/5mi).* It is another 20 mins. on foot from the carpark to the glacier. *Alpine Guides | Mount Cook | June–15 Oct 3 flights daily (equipment available for hire) | approx. 750 NZ$ (2 × 10km stretches and three circular flights, with a guide) | tel. 03 4 35 18 34 | www.alpineguides.co.nz | www.heliskiing.co.nz*

CHRIST-CHURCH

MAP INSIDE BACK COVER
(141 D5) *(🔖 F13)* **South Island's main metropolis (pop. 330,000) was changed completely on 22 February, 2011. An earthquake with a magnitude of 6.3**

CITY ▶ **WHERE TO START?**
Cathedral Square: When re-building work following the devastating earthquake in February 2011 has progressed enough and life returns to the centre, Cathedral Square will once again form the heart of the city. From here, all attractions in the centre can be reached on foot. The only tram line is purely used for sightseeing. All suburbs can be reached by bus as can the airport, which is some way out of town.

on the Richter Scale, with its epicentre near Lyttelton and just 6km (3¾mi) deep, destroyed buildings and the city's infrastructure, especially in the east. More than 180 people were killed.

The city centre around *Cathedral Square* simply buckled at the knees. Historical buildings included *Christ Church Cathedral* of 1864, *Canterbury Provincial Government Buildings* also in the Neogothic style, as well as *Canterbury Museum* and the *Arts Centre,* the time-honoured university that was later turned into a cultural centre with lots of studios, good restaurants and a lively craft market at weekends.

How much of the historical fabric can be saved and whether it is worth being rebuilt, remains to be seen. At the time of going to print, more than 900 buildings have to be demolished. This is a huge shame for this once intimate place, famous as a city of gardens, located on the fertile Canterbury Plains with a view of the mountain ranges rising to the west and with beautiful sandy beaches to the east. It will definitely take more than 10 years before it has recovered optically from the catastrophe and its infrastructure is back to normal. The tourist information office is closed, as are many pubs,

restaurants and hotels. For current information on progress being made see: *www.rebuildchristchurch.co.nz, www.chcheqjournal.com, www.canterburyearthquake.org.nz* and *www.cera.govt.nz.*

SIGHTSEEING

ART GALLERY

This modern glass building survived the hefty earthquake surprisingly well. When reopened, Old Masters and new works will be shown in temporary exhibitions. Interesting museum shop and café/restaurant with a terrace. *Worcester Blvd. | www.christchurchartgallery.org.nz*

ARTS CENTRE

This building from 1870 housed the University of Canterbury until 1970. Once comprehensive repair work has been completed, it should return to being a meeting place and cultural centre for the younger generation with cafés, bars and unusual art galleries. *Worcester Blvd./Rolleston Ave.*

BOTANIC GARDENS/HAGLEY PARK

Travel across Christchurch's green oasis in a canoe on the romantic Avon River. **INSIDER TIP** ▶ *Antigua Boat Sheds* with a café on a pretty terrace. *2 Cambridge Terrace | daily 9am–4.30pm | 15 NZ$/hours per canoe*

CANTERBURY MUSEUM

The damage here has been repaired relatively quickly and the collection reopened. This building, designed by Benjamin Mountfort, houses interesting exhibits on Maori culture, the exploration of the Antarctic from the early days until today, and the reconstruction of a road from colonial Christchurch. *Rolleston Ave. opposite the Arts Centre | daily 9am–5.30pm | admission free (donations appreciated) | www.canterburymuseum.com*

CHRIST CHURCH CATHEDRAL

Built in 1864 and badly damaged in the 2011 earthquake, the cathedral is to be preserved as a 'memorial' should it not be possible to rebuild it. Cathedral Square is the centre of the city where jugglers, tourists and locals meet in the summer.

(tel. 03 3 66 73 33 | www.christchurchinfo. co.nz). Daily 10am–4pm | 269 Bridle Path Rd. | www.ferrymead.org.nz

INTERNATIONAL ANTARCTIC CENTRE ●

A few minutes walks from the airport and 3800km (2360mi) from New Zealand's

A nostalgic chug around the Ferrymead Historic Park open-air museum

CHRIST'S COLLEGE

Well-known boys' public school. The school uniform is a grey pin-striped suit. *Rolleston Ave., next to Canterbury Museum | guided tours held occasionally*

FERRYMEAD HISTORIC PARK

Extensive open-air museum (focus on transport and fire service). Old steam engines and trams run in the park in the summer. In 1863 New Zealand's first steam engine was in Ferrymead. The museum is also a perfect setting for the *Tamuki Heritage Village* which takes a fascinating look back to the period around 1800 when there were many conflicts between the Maori and early settlers. The show, which is well worth seeing, is rounded off with a *hangi*

Scott Base in the Antarctic. Impressive exhibition on the Antarctic. *Oct–March daily 9am–8pm, April–Sept daily 9am–5.30pm | Orchard Rd. | www.iceberg.co.nz*

WIZARD

Officially a 'living work of art' who is now getting on a bit, the magician bewitches listeners on the Square with his philosophy about logic and the lack of it in everyday life. This former university professor's map of the world shows New Zealand and Australia right at the top, and Europe *down under* – a very popular souvenir (available in the i-SITE). The 2011 earthquake has also thrown him off course and sent him packing from Christchurch. But as soon as his open-air stage, Cathedral

A small lighthouse marks the entrance to the harbour in Akaroa – a little bit of France down under

Square, is open again, he'll be back *(irregularly at around 1pm)*.

FOOD & DRINK

INSIDER TIP POSEIDON
Great terrace on the beach, perfect for breakfast, lunch or tea. *25 The Esplanade | Sumner | tel. 03 3 26 70 90 | Moderate*

LEISURE & SPORTS

PUNTING ON THE AVON
Gondolieri will take you down the Avon River from the *Town Hall* or *Worcester St./ Oxford Terrace* jetty.

WHERE TO STAY

Almost half of the places to stay, especially in the centre, have been effected by the earthquake. For up-to-date lists of hotels, motels and backpacker hostels which are open, see *www.christchurchnz. com*

SUMNER MOTEL
Right in the middle of Sumner, Christchurch's lovely seaside suburb (20 min. drive, good bus connections) with pretty cafés, wonderful sandy beach and a promenade 1.5km (1mi) long. *12 rooms | 26 Marriner St. | tel. 03 3 26 59 69 | www. sumnermotel.co.nz | Moderate*

INFORMATION

CANTERBURY I-SITE
Find out at the *Visitor Information* in the international airport *(tel. 03 3 53 77 74)* or under *www.christchurchnz.net* as to its present location.

WHERE TO GO

BANKS PENINSULA
(141 D6) (𝄢 G13)

The attempt by the French on 11 February, 1840, to add New Zealand to their string of colonies is still being drawn upon today to attract tourists to the little town of ★ Akaroa with its French street signs and the historical *Langlois-Eteveneaux House (rue Lavaud/Balguerie | daily 10am–4.30pm | 8 NZ$)*. The Treaty of Waitangi between the British and the Maori had, however, already been in force for 5 days. The protected natural harbour bay is teeming with sea creatures. You can even INSIDER TIP swim with the dolphins *(Black Cat Cruises | Wainui Main Rd. | tel. 03 3 04 76 41 | www.blackcat.co.nz)* that play in the water. Lovely beaches can be found in Okains Bay, hotels and restaurants in the town and two wine-producing estates some 6–8km (4–5mi) to the west. *Visitor Information | 80 rue Lavand | tel. 03 3 04 86 00 | www.akaroa.com. 82km (50mi) southeast*

HANMER SPRINGS
(141 D4) (𝄢 G12)

A slightly sleepy but charming spa. The modern 38°C (100°F) *Thermal Pools (daily 10am–9pm | 12 NZ$)* offer a wide range of facilities *(www.hotfun.co.nz, www.hurunui.co.nz)*. *Heritage Hamner Springs (70 rooms | tel. 0800 36 88 88 | res@heritageho tels.co.nz | Moderate–Expensive)*, with a restaurant and small park, provides comfortable accommodation within easy walking distance. *135km (84mi) north*

LYTTELTON HARBOUR
(141 D5) (𝄢 F13)

New Zealand's most important harbour and South Island's economic backbone, as well as the home port of a Russian fishing fleet and the starting point of various major expeditions to the Antarctic. Since 1875, *The Timeball Station*, a castle-like structure above the harbour, has been signaling 1pm GMT to ships' crews. The historical building has first to be rebuilt following the earthquake in February 2011 as is the case with the whole of the little harbour town around London Street. The ☺ *farmers market* every Saturday morning selling local produce is very popular. A pretty fleamarket is often held next to it *(36 Oxford St.)*. A few miles away, in Governors Bay, INSIDER TIP *She Chocolate* conjures up chocolates and serves a delicious breakfast and brunch on the sunny terrace *(daily 10am–5pm | 79 Main Rd. | tel. 03 3 29 98 25 | Moderate)*. *5km (3mi) east*

SUMMIT ROAD ✂
(141 D5) (𝄢 F13)

Highly recommendable half-day tour across the *Port Hills* that separate Lyttelton from Christchurch. The first settlers had to drag their belongings over these hills in 1850. Drive through Cashmere to the restaurant *Sign of the Takahe (daily 10am–11am, 1.30pm–4pm)*, a good spot for a cup of tea, and *Sign of the Kiwi,* then up Summit Road (below the cablecar base station) and Evans Pass Road through the pretty resort Sumner and back via New Brighton. If you take the ✂ *Mt. Cavendish Gondola* up to a height of 446m (1463ft), you will have a wonderful view *(Hwy 74 to the road tunnel to Lyttelton, signposted | daily from 10am til late | www.gondola. co.nz | proposed re-opening around mid 2012)*.

The Summit Road is a spectacular route that can easily be done by mountainbike. *The Mountain Bike Adventure Co.* provides information on paths off the tarmaced road *(tel. 03 3 39 40 20 | www.cyclehire-tours.co.nz)*. *4km (2½mi) east*

TRANZALPINE EXPRESS 🍂

The 4½-hour train journey from Christchurch *(station in Addington | Clarence St. | departure 8.15am, arrival back in Christchurch 6pm)* to Greymouth (140 B4) *(ⅅ E12)* on the west coast, passes through the beautiful *Arthur's Pass. 209 NZ$ return trip | early booking through a travel agency recommended | tel. 0800 87 24 67 | www.tranzscenic.co.nz*

DUNEDIN

▧▧▧ **MAP INSIDE BACK COVER**
▧▧ (143 E4) *(ⅅ D16)* **A little piece of Scotland at the other end of the world. Founded by Scottish immigrants in 1848, it was given the Gaelic name for Edinburgh: Dunedin.**

'It's all right here', proclaims Dunedin's tourist authority and compares the city to Cologne and Cornwall, California and Cambridge, all in the same breath. Dunedin is the largest city in Otago, the region between the coast and Queenstown. Its wealth as a result of the goldrush in the 19th century can be seen in its magnificent buildings. Experts describe its as the best preserved Victorian town in the world. The lack of space in this hilly area forced residents to build their houses up the slopes too – an unusual urban planning decision for New Zealand towards the end of the 19th century.

Dunedin's economic success continued with the launching of the first refrigerator ship for the transport of fish in 1882 from Port Chalmers. The lucrative meat export business was ultimately monopolised by Christchurch. But Dunedin can be proud at being the native town of Thomas Bracken who wrote 'God Defend New Zealand', the text for New Zealand's national anthem.

SIGHTSEEING

STATION

Today, only the *Taieri Gorge Train (p. 78, 110)* departs from this station 1 or 2 times a day. That certainly helps to preserve the floor with pictures made using 725,760 mosaic tiles. The building erected in 1907 in the Flemish Renaissance style led to the architect George. A. Troup being given the nickname *Gingerbread George* – due to the building's façade. *Anzac Ave.*

BALDWIN STREET ●

With its 35% incline, this street has found its way into the Guinness Book of Records as the steepest residential road in the world over a length of 350m. The residents in this no-through-road get a little annoyed with tourists driving up it – but amazed pedestrians are welcome.

OLVESTON HOUSE

The house of the Theomin (1906) family is full of interesting artefacts and valuable Delftware. A good insight into how the wealthy lived around 1900. *42 Royal Terrace | daily 6 guided tours (advanced*

CITY **WHERE TO START?**
Octagon: Roads radiate in all directions from the Octagon (visitor centre), the city's central square. The northern section of George Street, the main thoroughfare that crosses the square, is the principle shopping street and stretches almost as far as the university. The most important sites can easily be reached from here on foot. For excursions to Otago Peninsula nearby, you will need wheels – bicycle ones will do too.

---

reservation necessary) | tel. 03 4 77 33 20 |
www.olveston.co.nz

INSIDER TIP ▶ OTAGO MUSEUM
Excellent exhibition on the life and culture in Southland: 'Southern Land – Southern People'. *419 Great King St. | daily 10am–5pm, guided tour daily 3.30pm (10 NZ$) | admission free, donations welcome | www.otagomuseum.govt.nz*

that is a good guide for an interesting tour around the city *(available at the i-SITE)*, starting from the Octagon.

FOOD & DRINK

Good pubs and nice restaurants can be found on the *Octagon*, in nearby *Moray Place* and *George Street (from the Octagon)*. The *Esplanade Restaurant* on

Dunedin's magnificent buildings are thanks to the gold-rush in the 19th century

UNIVERSITY OF OTAGO
17,000 students attend the oldest and best-known university in New Zealand – 10% of Dunedin's residents. A stroll through the campus will take you past the Clock Tower in the Gothic Revival style. *Leith St.*

WALK THE CITY
35 historical buildings in the *City of Grace and Grandeur* are described in a brochure

lovely INSIDER TIP ▶ *St Clair Beach* can be recommended for tasty lunches and dinners *(Mediterranean cuisine | 5/250 Forbury Road | tel. 03 4 56 25 44 | Moderate)*.

BACCHUS WINE BAR
Good wines, light meals and imaginative menu. *Mon–Sat lunch/dinner | 12 The Octagon | tel. 03 4 74 08 24 | Moderate*

MAZAGRAN ESPRESSO BAR
Drop in for that special coffee experience and the lovely smell of freshly ground beans. *36 Moray Place*

LEISURE & SPORTS

TAIERI GORGE RAILWAY
Fancy a trip to Queenstown *(142 C3)* *(₥ C15)* with a difference? Then take this 2-hour train ride in a historical carriage through the luxuriant countryside of Otago and spectacular gorges to Pukerangi, and then travel the remaining 4 hours or so by bus *(130 NZ\$, return train journey only 80 NZ\$ | Oct–March daily 2.30pm, otherwise 12.30pm, also 9.30am in the high season | tel. 03 477 44 49 | www.taieri.co.nz).*

WHERE TO STAY

INSIDER TIP NISBET COTTAGE
Cosy B&B with a wonderful breakfast and a hostess who, as a biologist, knows everything about the natural environment. Guided tours available *(www.nznatureguides.com). 3 rooms | 6a Elliffe Place | tel. 03 454 5169 | Moderate*

MOTEL ON YORK
Well-presented rooms, near the Octagon and George Street (restaurants). *23 rooms | 47 York Place | tel. 03 477 6120 | www.motelonyork.co.nz | Moderate*

INFORMATION

DEPARTMENT OF CONSERVATION
Brochure on *Otago Goldfields Heritage Hwy* available *(www.goldfieldstrust.org.nz). 77 Lower Stuart St. | tel. 03 477 06 77*

DUNEDIN I-SITE
48 The Octagon | tel. 03 474 33 00 | www.dunedinnz.com | www.dunedin.govt.nz

WHERE TO GO

INSIDER TIP THE CATLINS
(142–143 C–D5) (₥ C–D 16–17)
Untamed forests, idyllic waterfalls and lonely bays – the Catlins between Invercargill and Balclutha are still one of New Zealand's real insider's tips. One special attraction is a petrified, ● 170 million-year-old forest in Curio Bay *(Jurassic Petrified Forest)*, that can be seen at low tide. You can also watch the seals, sea lions and yellow-eyed penguins. An ideal, basic place to stay is *Curio Bay Camping Ground (tel. 03 246 88 97 or 03 246 84 43 | Budget)* just 100m away. The brochure *Southern Scenic Route*, available at the i-SITE in Dunedin describes a tour you can take *(www.catlins.org.nz). Catlins Wildlife Trackers* in Papatowai *(tel. 03 415 86 13 | www.catlins-ecotours.co.nz)* organise tours over several days as well as accommodation. An old bus forms the centrepiece of the *Lost Gypsy Gallery* where Blair Summerville exhibits his wonderfully eccentric objects *(Thu–Tue 11am–5pm | 5 NZ\$ | tel. 03 415 89 08).* Self-caterers can stay in the depths of the country between the sea and the rainforest at *Southern Secret Motel (Papatowai Hwy | tel. 03 415 86 00 | Moderate).* In the north of the Catlins, near exposed *Nugget Lighthouse*, *Nugget Lodge* has two flats with a view of the ocean and an unforgetable sunrise *(367 The Nuggets Rd. | tel. 03 412 87 83 | www.nuggetlodge.co.nz | Moderate–Expensive). 120km (75mi) south*

MOERAKI BOULDERS
(143 F3) (₥ E15)
80km (50mi) north of Dunedin, on Hwy 1, huge boulders with a circumference of up to 4m, sit on the beach. According to geologists, these 'stone bubbles' of fine crystals were created more than 4 million years ago through volcanic activity. There

The Moeraki Boulders: 4 million years old and with a diameter of up to 4m (13ft)

is a café above the beach. Don't miss out on a visit to **INSIDER TIP** *Fleur's Place*, a fantastic fish restaurant with its own smoking chamber, located about 1km (½mi) away in Moeraki Village next to the old jelly. Try *muttonbird*, a Maori delicacy *(lunch/dinner | tel. 03 4 39 44 80 | Moderate)*. A campsite with reasonably priced cabins is within eyeshot *(tel. 03 4 39 47 59 | www.moerakivillageholiday park.co.nz | Budget)*.

OAMARU
(143 F3) (*ⁿ E15*)

The many impressive buildings made of gleaming white limestone are testimony to a wealthy past when frozen meat was exported throughout the world from the harbour here. A patina now lies over the town, 115km (72mi) north of Dunedin; the extra-wide main street seems lifeless, the harbour is deserted. But life has re-turned to the former warehouses and business premises: **INSIDER TIP** *Harbour Tyne Historic Precinct* is home to unusual art galleries, a motor museum, original grocery stores and idiosyncratic gastron-omy. Potent brews can be sampled in the *NZ Malt Whiskey Company (daily 10am–5pm | 14 Harbour St. | tel. 03 4 34 88 42)*. Guided tours also available *(15 NZ$)*.

Not far away, a colony of little blue pen-guins provides an insight into their eve-ryday life. The best time is at dusk when the animals return from a day at sea *(daily from 9am | 20 NZ$ | Visitor Centre | Waterfront Rd. | www.penguins.co.nz)*. The restaurant *Casa Nova House (1 Alt St. | tel. 03 4 37 17 82 | Moderate)* can be recom-mended. Good leaflets on the *Arts and Crafts Trail* and *Explore Historic Oamaru* are available from the *Information Centre/i-SITE (1 Thames St. | tel. 03 4 34 16 56 | www.visitoamaru.co.nz)*.

OTAGO PENINSULA ★
(143 E4) (*Ø E16*)

You should plan at least one day for this magical peninsula near Dunedin with its gently undulating park-like scenery. The first Maori settlement on the peninsula was at Otakou, which the Europeans adapted to Otago. The narrow road, that winds its way 60km (37mi) along the coast of the promontory, ends at *Taia-roa Head* where the only ● mainland colony of albatrosses and have a wingspan of around 3.5m (11½ft), is shown on a video in the information center.

Opposite the centre a path leads to *Natures Wonders Otago (tel. 0800 24 64 46 / www. natureswondersnaturally.com)*. Small off-road vehicles will take you to beaches where there are penguins and seals. Alternatively, visit Howard McGrouther and his *Penguin Place (daily up to ten 90-min. guided tours / 35 NZ$ / tel. 03 4 78*

A thrilling hike lets you explore the fascinating world of Fox Glacier

can be seen. Seals, penguins and cormorants also feel at home here. With a bit of luck and a pair of binoculars, you can watch pairs of birds during the breeding season between Nov and Jan in the albatross colony *(24 Nov–16 Sept / 40 NZ$ / tel. 03 4 78 04 99 / www.albatross.org.nz)*. Chicks hatch in Jan and Feb and are fed by their parents in the nest for the first 100 days. What you may not be able to see as a visitor to the colony of these huge seabirds, which weight up to 8kg (17½lbs)

02 86 / www.pengiunplace.co.nz) where you can see the yellow-eyed penguin at close quarters. As visitors have to move along narrow tunnels hidden under netting, you will not be noticed by the shy animals. The best time to penguin watch is in the late afternoon *(last guided tour approx. 90 min. before sunset)*.

☆ *Larnach Castle,* New Zealand's only castle, is a beautifully restored, imposing and bleak building that was constructed at great expense between 1873 and 1886 by the banker William Larnach using building materials from Italy and Scotland. The former sheep building is now a ballroom *(daily 9am–5pm | 25 NZ$ | www.larnach castle.co.nz)*. You can stay near the castle at *Larnach Castle Lodge,* and houseguests may eat in the elegant dining room *(tel. 03 476 16 16 | www.larnachcastle.co.nz | Moderate–Expensive)*. There is a small campsite in Portobello that is popular in the high season. General information on the peninsula can be found under *www. otago-peninsula.co.nz*

FRANZ JOSEF

(140 A5) (*ṁ D13*) The little village on the west coast (on SH 6) was named after the Austrian Emperor by the geologist Julius von Haast.

There are few places to stay here, but it is a good starting point for a visit to the *Franz Josef Glacier (book accommodation a few days in advance between Nov and March!)*. Good information board at the ☆☆ glacier terminal *(13km/8mi away)* with details of the history and dimensions of the glacier. The glacier, at present 11km (6¾mi) long, grows and shrinks. The walk to the ice from the carpark may therefore vary too, but takes at least an hour.

WEST COAST WILDLIFE CENTRE

The breeding station focuses on the rarest species of kiwi, the *rowi,* that is only found in this region. At the most there are only 400 of these birds still living in the wild. If you buy a *Backstage Kiwi Pass (40 NZ$)* you can join a guided tour through the hatchery. A café and bread shop on the corner of Cowan/Cron St. is open to all visitors. *Daily 9am–8pm | tel. 03 752 06 00 | www.westcoastwildlifecentre.co.nz*

LEISURE & SPORTS

GLACIER FLIGHTS ★ ☆☆

Depending on the weather, glacier hikes are available, also at Fox Glacier, as a packet with a helicopter flight *(Helihikes | 399 NZ$ for 4 hours | tel. 0800 80 77 67 | www.foxguides.co.nz)*. Three companies offer trips by plane *(between 190 and 380 NZ$, sometimes cheaper stand-by tickets available | tel. 0800 80 77 67 | www.heli copter.co.nz)*. Please note: after landing on the glacier the aeroplane pilots turn the engines off, the helicopter pilots leave them running – which some people might find really irritating in such magnificent surroundings. In the *Imax Theatre* in the *Alpine Adventure Centre* the mountains can be seen from the air on a colossal screen *(6 shows daily)*. Sightseeing flights also take off from Lake Tekapo. *Other organisers can be found in the centre on the main street*

GLACIER HOT POOLS

This bathing paradise surrounded by dense vegetation can only do you good after a chilly glacier hike. Just lie back in one of the various hot pools and let yourself be massaged. *Daily noon–10pm | Cron St. | tel. 0800 04 40 44 | from 25 NZ$ | www.glacierhotpools.co.nz*

WHERE TO STAY

TE WAONUI FOREST RETREAT ☺

This elegant hotel has been integrated perfectly into the environment. Sheets are made of organically grown cotton and recycled building materials keep the ecologically-minded happy. Gourmets can enjoy their food between trees in the restaurant *The Canopy. 100 rooms | 3 Wallace St. | tel. 03 357 19 19 or 0800 69 69 63 | www.scenichotelgroup.co.nz | Expensive (from 700 NZ$)*

RAINFOREST HOLIDAY PARK

Much cheaper than in the Retreat is, of course, the campsite opposite. *46 Cron St. | opposite Hot Pools | tel. 03 752 02 20 | www.rainforestholidaypark.co.nz | Budget*

INFORMATION

WESTLAND NATIONAL PARK HEADQUARTERS

Very good ranger station with elaborate displays on the 60 glaciers in Westland National Park and the rain forest. *Tel. 03 752 07 96 | www.west-coast.co.nz*

WHERE TO GO

FOX GLACIER ☼
(140 A5) (*ɱ D13*)

The slightly smaller glacier, 25km (15½mi) from Franz Josef. Sightseeing flights also take off from here, depending on the weather.

HAAST PASS
(143 D1–2) (*ɱ C14*)

Named after the German geologist and naturalist Julius von Haast (1822–87). The low pass divides the raw rainy west coast from mild Central Otago. The building of the road – an old Maori trail – took more than 10 years. *South Westland World Heritage Visitor Centre, SH 6 | daily 9am–6pm, April–Nov 9am–4.30pm. 140km (87mi) south*

LAKE MATHESON ☼
(140 A5) (*ɱ D13*)

Whoever drives to the lake early in the morning when the weather is clear, and then walks the 30 minutes to the viewpoint with the appropriate name *View of Views*, really will be rewarded with a breathtaking vista of Lake Matheson and the mountain peaks mirrored in it. *32km (20mi) southwest*

LAKE MOERAKI
(143 D1) (*ɱ C13*)

Tours to the penguin colonies and hikes through the largest protected rainforest in New Zealand on Lake Moeraki are offered by experienced guides at the *Lake Moeraki Wilderness Lodge (SH 6 | tel. 03 750 08 81 | www.wildernesslodge. co.nz | Moderate–Expensive). 100km (62mi) south*

LAKE PARINGA (143 D1) (*ɱ C13*)

Half way between Fox Glacier and Haast Pass you can buy **INSIDER TIP** fantastic salmon – either fresh or smoked. *SH 6, Lake Paringa. 80km (50mi) south*

INSIDER TIP ▶ **OKARITO** 140 A5) (🗺 *D13*)
This little place with just a handful of houses is on a promontory in a lagoon and is surrounded by the tempestuous Tasman Sea, thick rainforest and the frequently snowcapped mountains of the Southern Alps. A good 30 people live in this former gold mining township, including the famous New Zealand writer Keri Hulme *(The Bone People)*. Visitors however come here every day in their hundreds to marvel at the wild sections of beach littered with driftwood or to watch *brown kiwis (tours after sunset: www.okaritokiwi tours.co.nz)* between Okarito and Franz Josef 30km (19mi) away. The rare *great white heron (kotuku)* can be spotted on a boat-trip across the lagoon. The historic *Okarito Schoolhouse* opposite the campsite, a unique hostel that is known well beyond the country's borders, has 12 beds in two rooms *(closed in winter | www. okarito.net | Budget)*.

GREYMOUTH

(140 B4) (🗺 *E12*) **Greymouth (pop. 8000) is the economic hub of the West Coast that extends 500km (310mi) from above Westport in the north to beyond Haast Pass in the south.**

Tasman Sea, Southern Alps and dense rainforest skirt Okarito Lagoon

In between, the rough Tasman Sea washes the coastal plain that is bordered by high cliffs. Nowhere in West Coast is wider than 50km (31mi). Glaciers and rainforest – where else in the world are such contrasts so close together? The long periods of heavy rain are a feature of the region. Drivers must be careful: there are still several single-track bridges (even also shared with trains!). And roads in the rainforest can quickly turn into slippery slides. Those who live here have all the time in the world. You should plan at least three days for the journey along the wonderful coastline stopping off at Greymouth, Hokitika and Franz Josef. Greymouth can also be reached by the TranzAlpine Express – the train back to Christchurch leaves around noon.

SIGHTSEEING

SHANTYTOWN

Very well designed open-air museum with furnished houses from gold-digging days. With a bit of luck, you may recuperate the cost of the lesson in gold panning *(25 NZ$)* by finding a nugget or two! *8km (5mi) south of Greymouth, signposted | daily 8.30am–5pm*

FOOD & DRINK

Try a glass of local beer: Monteiths comes in large bottles with swing top stops. The brewery can also be visited: *daily 11.30am, 2pm, 4pm, 6pm, 7pm | corner Turumaha/ Herbert St. | www.monteiths.co.nz*

Open-air 'shanty town': pan for gold, shop and sleep like the gold-diggers of old

SHOPPING

IAN BOUSTRIDGE

Ian Boustridge works extremely hard New Zealand greenstone *(Pounamu)* with incomparable artistic skill, drawing his inspiration from Maori motifs. If you ring up in advance, you can watch him working in his studio a few miles south of Greymouth *(Ortsteil Paroa | Unit 7 | 56 Jacks Road | tel. 03 768 60 48 | www.ian boustridge.com)*.

INFORMATION

GREYMOUTH I-SITE

Mackay/Herbert St. | tel. 03 768 51 01 | Hotel reservations through the Greymouth

Information Centre | www.westcoast.co.nz, www.westcoastnz.com

WHERE TO GO

ARTHUR'S PASS
(140 C4–5) *(E–F12)*
Incredibly beautiful stretch through the national park of the same name and over the Alps, past Mt. Murchison (2400m/ 7900ft) on Hwy 73 to Christchurch. Information under *www.selwyn.govt.nz. 256km (160mi), 4 hours by car*

PUNAKAIKI
(140 B–C3) *(E11)*
Paparoa National Park boasts geological features created by erosion over a period of 30 million years with layered limestone formations – ● *Pancake Rocks* – shaped by the power of the waves. Tip: after 4.30pm you'll have this magnificent scenery virtually to yourself. In the little village on the SH 6 there is an excellent craft shop *(daily 9am–7pm)*, a visitor centre *(www.punakaiki.co.nz)* with interesting displays and a good campsite *(Punakaiki Beach Camp | tel. 03 731 18 94)* as well as a cosy pub-restaurant built like a log cabin. *70km (43½mi) north*

REEFTON
(140 C3) *(F11)*
Gold was once mined in this town where the first electric street light in the southern hemisphere was switched on in 1888, as the exhibition in *Black's Point Museum* clearly explains *(Aug–May Tue–Sun 1pm– 4pm | 7 NZ$). 80km (50mi) northeast*

WESTPORT (140 C3) *(E11)*
The interesting *Coaltown Museum* with sound effects is housed in an old brewery in this otherwise rather dull little town *(daily 9am–4.30pm | Queen St. | 7 NZ$). Tauranga Bay*, 12km (7½mi) away, is home

to the most northerly colony of seals in New Zealand *(viewing platform on Tauranga Bay Rd., off the SH6 to the north of Westport or via Hwy 67A from Westport)*. The pleasant INSIDERTIP *Bay House Café (Tauranga Bay | tel. 03 789 71 33 | www.thebayhouse.co.nz)* is closeby.

A further 90km (56mi) to the north, sleepy little *Karamea* enjoys a subtropical microclimate made for relaxing. You can also visit one or other karst cave, e.g. *Honeycomb Hill Caves & Arch,* only accessible as part of a guided tour *(Oparara Guided Tours | 75 NZ$ | tel. 03 782 66 52, www.oparara.co.nz)*. Information under *www.westport.org.nz. 85km (53mi) north*

HOKITIKA

(140 B4) (*ᗰ E12*) **Once the provincial capital, this popular shopping centre has developed into an important tourist resort.**

One of the town's most famous sons is Richard Seddon, who set up the first pension scheme. A memorial to the former Prime Minister is in Sewell St. Every year in early March, the *Wildfoods Festival (www.wildfoods.co.nz)* is held in Hokitika.

FOOD & DRINK

CAFÉ DE PARIS
Modern New Zealand cuisine. *lunch/dinner daily | 19 Tancred St. | tel. 03 755 89 33 | Moderate*

SHOPPING

Most shops (toys made of rimu wood, gold jewellery and glass) are on Tancred St. and are open every day. Original ● items made of jade can be found in *Mountain Jade (corner Weld/Sewell St.)*, at *Tectonic Jade (Revell St.)*, *Traditional Jade (diagonally opposite the visitor information)* and in the *Craft Gallery (25 Tancred St.)*. You can even make INSIDERTIP your own jewellery out of jade *(taonga)*, bone or *paua* under expert supervision in *Bonz 'n' Stonz*. Courses last 2–8 hours and cost between 55–95 NZ$. *16 Hamilton St. | tel. 03 755 65 04 | www.bonz-n-stonz.co.nz*

IN TOLKIEN COUNTRY

Since the film premiere of 'The Lord of the Rings' based on J.R.R. Tolkien's novels, a 'Middle-earth' tourist boom has set in. Let yourself be wooed by the unique scenery on South Island featured in the fantasy epic, e.g. in Arrowtown, where the Arrow River bed was used as the Ford of Bruinen. This is where Arwen used his magical power to cause a flood, killing the horses of the Ringwraiths. Tolkein's Anduin River with its mighty pillars is the Kawarau River (rafting tours with *Extreme Green Rafting | 39 Camp St. | tel. 03 442 85 17)*. A particular highlight is to ride to where the Amon Hen and Nan Curunir scenes were filmed, the valley of Saruman – even with no riding experience *(Dart Stables | Glenorchy | tel. 0800 474 34 64)*. Other locations are shown on an off-road 'Safari of the Rings' tour *(Nomad Safaris | tel. 0800 68 82 22 | www.nomadsafaris.co.nz)*. In 2011, Peter Jackson began filming 'The Hobbit' in two parts (premieres in Dec 2012 and 2013). And then there will be a lot more secret locations to see.

The subtropical climate is made for relaxing, like here on the banks of the Kohaihai River

WHERE TO STAY

BEACHFRONT HOTEL

Right in the centre just a few yards from the wild West Coast beach. Rooms with seaviews. *68 rooms | Revell St. | tel. 03 755 83 44 | www.beachfronthotel.co.nz | Moderate*

INFORMATION

WESTLAND VISITOR INFORMATION

The leaflet *Gold Panning on the West Coast* provides tips how and where you can seek your fortune. *Corner Tancred/Hamilton St. | tel. 03 755 61 66 | www.hokitika.org*

WHERE TO GO

ROSS (140 B4) (*⬙ E12*)

Gold-diggers can still be found today on the Coast. The mine opposite the *Empire Hotel (Aylmer St. | daily from noon | tel.* *03 755 40 05 | Budget)*, built in 1866, was only closed in 2004. There are some 90 licence holders digging for gold in this area today. Several trails tracing the golden past start at the hotel (e.g. the easy 2km/1¼mi-long *Water Race Walk*). And if you fancy a try yourself, the visitor information *(daily 9am–4pm | tel. 03 755 40 77)* has gold-digging gear for hire. *30km (19mi) southwest*

NELSON

(141 E2) (*⬙ G10*) **The country's fifth largest town (pop. 50,000) rather cockily calls itself the 'Sunshine Capital' of New Zealand. Nowhere in New Zealand does the sun shine as much or is the climate as pleasant as here in the north of South Island.**

The lifestyle of the locals correspondingly matches this: laid back, focussing

Roses and bonvivants blossom in Nelson's mild climate

on the nicer things in life. Nelson and the surrounding area is home to artists and bonvivants. This is where not only delicious fruit and some of the best vines grow, it is also where there are beautiful beaches and fantastic hiking possibilities in Abel Tasman National Park.

SIGHTSEEING

THE SUTER ART GALLERY

Works by local and international 19th and 20th-century artists. Good café. *Daily 10am–5pm | 208 Bridge St. | entrance fee 4 NZ$ | www.thesuter.org.nz*

WOW

Wearable Art is the name of the annual event in Wellington at which imaginative fashion is displayed and prizes awarded. The most adventurous items are on show in the *World of Wearable Art* (WOW). There is also an oldtimer collection in the same building. *Daily 10am–6pm | 95 Quarantine Rd. near the airport | 15 NZ$ | www.wowcars.co.nz*

FOOD & DRINK

THE HONEST LAWYER

Cosy 'olde worlde' English-style pub. Good fish and meat dishes, beer garden on the water. Rooms furnished in country style *(Moderate–Expensive)*. *1 Point Rd. Monaco (15 min. towards Richmond) | tel. 03 5 47 88 50 | www.honestlawyer.co.nz | Moderate–Expensive*

NELSON WATERFRONT

The choice becomes difficult here as a number of excellent fish restaurants *(Boat Shed, Harbourlight, Saltwater)* have established themselves along the (congested) waterfront in Nelson *(268–351 Wakefield Quay)*. A good tip for self-caterers: *Guytons Fresh Fish (270 Wakefield Quay)*. And excellent fish 'n chips can be found next door at *Haven*.

SHOPPING

A craft fair is held every Saturday on Montgomery Place *(8am–noon)*. The choice is smaller on Sun.

JENS HANSEN

The Hansen's in Nelson are the true 'lords of the ring' as it was here that the prototype of the magic gold ring was made for the trilogy 'Lord of the Rings', filmed in New Zealand, that was first screened in 2001. *320 Trafalger Square | www.jens hansen.com*

LEISURE & SPORTS

SWIMMING

The best beaches are *Tahunanui Beach* (near Nelson, with a campsite), on *Rabbit Island* on the Waimea River *(turn off Hwy 60 after Upper Moutere)* and near *Kaiteriteri* in Abel Tasman National Park.

WHERE TO STAY

CATHEDRAL INN

This cosy B&B is right next to the cathedral. *369 Trafalgar St. | South | tel. 03 5 48 73 69 | www.cathedralinn.co.nz | Moderate*

INSIDER TIP SOUTH STREET COTTAGES

Some of the beautifully restored buildings on South Street close to the centre are now cosy guesthouses. Reservation absolutely essential! *Tel. 03 5 40 27 69 | www. cottageaccommodation.co.nz | Moderate– Expensive*

INFORMATION

VISITOR INFORMATION

Corner Trafalgar/Halifax St. | tel. 03 5 48 23 04 | www.nelsonnz.com

WHERE TO GO

ABEL TASMAN NATIONAL PARK ★
(141 D1) *(ꕤ G10)*

Named after the Dutchman who was the first European to set eyes on the coast of New Zealand in 1642. As the Maori attacked his ship, he quickly sailed off without setting foot on the island.

That's a pity, as he would certainly have appreciated the wonderful scenery here.

LOW BUDGET

▶ You only need sturdy shoes and a torch for this exciting do-it-yourself cave tour through *Punakaiki Caves* on the west coast *(5 mins. from the DOC Visitor Centre on the SH 6 | www.punakaiki.co.nz)*.

▶ Mini dinos in *Southland Museum* in Invercargill: visit the *tuataras,* as this ancient and rare lizard-like reptile is called – it's free *(Mon–Fri 9am–5pm, Sat/Sun 10am–5pm | 108 Gala St. | www.southland museum.com)*.

▶ As most tourists with campervans travel from Auckland to Christchurch, many who have rented vehicles need 'relocation drivers' to get it back to North Island again. Find out more 2–3 weeks beforehand *(e.g. Maui Rentals | tel. 09 2 55 06 20 | nzrelocsonline@thlonline.com)*.

The national park covers more than 85mi² of almost uninterrupted forest with Nikau palms and giant ferns as well as South Sea-like beaches of fine sand that are popular between December and March. Water taxis ply the stretch between *Kaiteriteri* and *Totaranui* (lovely grassy campsite with a long beach, no electricity hook-ups). That means that the coastal track – easily walkable in 4–5 days – can be split into day excursions. Reservations

Moderate) are well positioned on a slope. There are more hotels and restaurants in *Motueka*. **INSIDER TIP** *Awaroa Lodge (250 NZ$/doubles | 26 rooms | tel. 03 5 28 87 58 | www.awaroalodge.co.nz)* lies hidden in the dense vegetation in the park. If this is too expensive, you should at least take take a water taxi and go there for lunch and a walk along the fantastic beach. A kajak trip down the coast is a safe adventure *(p. 109)*.

A must for water-loving hikers: a tour through Abel Tasman National Park

for the boats are necessary *(e.g. Abel Tasman Enterprises | 265 High St. | Motueka | tel. 0800 22 35 82 | www.abeltasmannz. com | trips: daily 8.45am from the campsite on the beach at Kaiteriteri; 9am from Marahau Beach). Park Café (at the Marahau Beach park entrance | daily 8am–10pm)* can be recommended. The nearby *Ocean View Chalets (10 rooms | tel. 03 5 27 82 32 |*

Information: *Motueka i-SITE | Wallace St. | tel. 03 5 28 65 43 | www.nelsonnz.com/ motueka. 80km (50mi) northwest*

GOLDEN BAY
(141 D1) (*F F–G 9–10*)
An inviting, crescent-shaped bay with soft golden sand seems made for a swim and a stroll along the beach – unless of course

there is a warm nor'westerly blowing that can whip up the waves across Cook Strait. *Takaka* is the main centre with a number of shops. To the west is the world's largest freshwater spring: the *Waikoropupu* or *Pupu Springs* for short, spew out 14,000 litres a second. The clear water may be inviting but neither swimming nor diving are allowed. The footpath from the carpark leads to a viewpoint *(Pupu Springs Rd.).* In *Collingwood* off-road safaris head for INSIDER TIP *Farewell Spit*, the uninhabited promontory at the northern end of the bay that consists almost entirely of huge sand dunes. This is paradise for countless colonies of birds *(approx. 6 hours | Farewell Spit Safari | tel. 03 5 24 82 57 | www.fare wellspit.co.nz).*

Just inland from the bay, ambitious hikers set off on the 77km (48mi)-long *Heaphy Track* (5–6 days) through the *Kahurangi National Park* on the west coast. 😊 *Sans Souci Inn* with a grass roof and organic garden is a charming place to stay with a Mediterranean flair. Bathroom facilities (incl. composting WCs) are shared by all guests *(7 rooms | Pohara | Richmond Rd. | tel. 03 5 25 86 63 | www.sanssouciinn. co.nz | Budget–Moderate).* 170km (106mi) northwest

NELSON LAKES NATIONAL PARK
(141 D3) (*ω F–G11*)
St Arnaud on Lake Rotoiti is a small tourist resort and starting point for hikes through the mountainous national park. The envigorating *Honeydew Walk* along the lakeside takes less than one hour. The solid log cabins at *Nelson Lakes Motel (Main Rd. | tel. 03 5 21 18 87 | www.nelson lakes.co.nz | Budget)* have been well integrated into the mountain scenery. Anglers and hunters will find perfect conditions around Lake Rotorua and Lake Rotoiti. Eels can weigh around 2kg, brown trout 2½kg. *Boris Cech* in St Arnaud is an in-

formative guide *(tel. 03 5 43 91 21).* The best time to fish is Oct–April – although the sandflies are particularly bloodthirsty then. *100km (62mi) southwest*

UPPER MOUTERE
(141 D2) (*ω G10*)
This is the fruit-growing area with a variety of wonderful apples and vines. Upper Moutere (pron. 'Mutri') was founded in 1843 by Germans as can be seen in the small graveyard. Local wines can be sampled in *Seifried* winery *(daily 10am–5pm | corner Hwy 60/Redwood Rd. | Appleby). 22km (14mi) west*

PICTON

(141 E–F2) (*ω H10*) **The 'Gateway to South Island' is a rather dull town which wakes up briefly when the ferries come in.**

The wistful memory of 1865, when Picton wanted to become the capital, is little consolation. The nicest spot is ◿ *Queen Charlotte Drive* which leads to Havelock. The route winds around the bays along Marlborough Sounds – especially appealing for caravaners. *Mgakuta Bay* in the soft late afternoon light is like a fairy tale. The turning at Link Water takes you along a tarmaced but twisty road to Kenepuru Sound and Portage. INSIDER TIP *Te Mahia Bay Resort* with lovely rooms is in a romantic location on the water *(tel. 03 5 73 40 89 | www.temahia.co.nz | Moderate).*

FOOD & DRINK

Nice cafés with good lunches and dinners can be found on the High Street *(The Quest, Cibo and Dog & Frog Café).* ◿ *Le Café*, right in the middle on London Quay with a view of the marina can also be recommended.

PICTON

Whale-hunting off the coast of Kaikoura – with the camera, that is

WHERE TO STAY

MCCORMICK HOUSE
Charming B&B in a house built in 1914 with a wonderful garden and attentive hosts. *3 rooms | 2km (1¼mi) from Picton | 21 Leicester St. | tel. 03 573 52 53 | www. mccormickhouse.co.nz | Expensive*

HARBOUR VIEW HOTEL
Centrally located motel with a lovely view of the harbour. *12 rooms | Waikawa Rd. | tel. 03 573 62 59 | www.harbourview picton.co.nz | Moderate*

INFORMATION

PICTON I-SITE
The Foreshore (on the jetty) | tel. 03 573 74 77. The *Department of Conservation*

(tel. 03 573 75 82 | www.destination marlborough.com, www.picton.co.nz) is in the same building

WHERE TO GO

BLENHEIM (141 E2) *(⌗ H10–11)*
This is actually the centre of Marlborough and the heart of New Zealand's most extensive wine-growing area. A large wine and food festival *(p. 120)* is held at *Montana Wines,* the biggest producer here. The winery is south of Blenheim on the SH1 *(Mon–Sat 10am–3pm, 20 min. guided tours).*
The ★ *Marlborough Wine Trail* (leaflet available at Picton i-SITE) takes you to the best wine-growers in the region that are mostly along *Rapaura Rd.* You can sample the wine at many of them *(beyond*

Renwick turn off the SH 6 onto Rapaura Rd. before Wairau River).

The best lunches are served every day in ● INSIDER TIP *La Veranda (Vintage Lane | Renwick | tel. 03 5 72 72 30 | Moderate)* on *Georges Michel's* wine-growing estate. Olives, ice cream and brandy are sold at *Taste of Marlborough (Papaura Rd.). 15km (9½mi) south*

KAIKOURA ★
(141 E4) (*ftl G12*)

This little town 120km (75mi) south of Picton is well known largely as a place for watching whales and dolphins. The best time to see these marine animals is Oct–April.

A trip to the whales costs 150 NZ$ *(Whale Watch Kaikoura | Railway Station | tel. 0800 65 51 21 | www.whalewatch.co.nz)* or to the dolphins *(Kaikoura Dolphin Encounter | West End | tel. 03 3 19 67 77 | www.dolphin.co.nz)*. And that comes with a guarantee – if you don't see any whales you get 80% of the price refunded.

On the edge of the village, not far from the fishing harbour, is a small colony of seals *(Seal Colony | Fyffe Quay)* that is within easy walking distance. In Kaikoura, which means 'crayfish feast' in Maori, and in the surrounding area, fresh or cooked crayfish can be bought everywhere *(e.g. at Nin's Bin | Hwy 1, 23km/14mi) north of Kaikoura).* Information: *Visitor Information | Kaikoura | Memorial Hall | West End | tel. 03 3 19 56 41 | www.kaikoura.co.nz*

MARLBOROUGH SOUNDS ☼
(141 E–F 1–2) (*ftl G–H10*)

This confusing mass of bays with dense vegetation on the slopes, once settled by the Maori and the subject of many a legend, combined with the narrow beaches (along a 900km/560mi stretch of coastline) can be easily explored by boat. The cheaper alternativie, but just as interest-ing, is to take the Mail Boat. Day trips by boat are also available to the beautiful *Queen Charlotte Track (www.qctrack.co.nz)*. The best area for hikes is between *Ship Cove* and *Furneaux Lodge. Magic Mail Run from Picton Mon–Sat 1.30pm to Ship Cove | approx. 4 hours for 100 NZ$; Beachcomber Fun Cruise | tel. 03 5 73 61 75 | www.beachcombercruises.co.nz*

QUEENS-TOWN

(142 C3) (*ftl C15*) ★ For some it is a fascinating adventure playground, others criticise the flood of tourists descending on this little place.

The masses however soon get spread out in Queenstown that, despite its popularity in summer and winter, still retains the charm of a modest resort on romantic Lake Wakatipu. Queenstown also poses a few questions: why for example does the level of the water in the lake 115mi² rise and fall some 12cm every few minutes? Because of the heartbeat of the giant living at the bottom – according to the Maori myth. In fact the reason is the change in atmospheric pressure due to the cold and hot air that passes over the lake.

SIGHTSEEING

BOB'S PEAK ☼

From here you have a breathtaking view over Lake Wakatipu. The more adventurous have a choice between bungee jumping and the fast tarmac luge run; or else you can glide down into the valley on a tandem paraglide jump *(approx. 205 NZ$ | for names of companies visit the i-SITE or ask locally | tel. 0800 75 96 88 | www.paraglide.net.nz). Cablecar terminal on Brecon St.*

QUEENSTOWN

GIBBSTON VALLEY WINE
One of the most southerly wineries in the world doesn't need to worry about competition. Good lunches, excellent cheeses. *Daily 10am–5pm | SH 6, a short distance from Kawarau Bridge towards Cromwell | tel. 03 4 42 69 10 | www.gvwines.co.nz*

FOOD & DRINK

INSIDERTIP THE BATH HOUSE
Tapas are served in this restaurant in a former changing hut right on the lake. Lovely terrace. *Lunch/dinner daily | tel. 03 4 42 56 25 | Moderate*

BOARDWALK
The best tip for fish dishes in Queenstown. *Lunch/dinner daily | Steamer Wharf Village | Beach St. | tel. 03 4 42 56 30 | Expensive*

BOTSWANA BUTCHERY ☙
Indulge in meat dishes inspired by South African cuisine in this restaurant with a view over Lake Wakatipu. Not cheap but reliably good. Reservation essential – in good weather outside on the terrace. *17 Marine Parade | tel. 03 4 42 69 94 | www.goodbars.co.nz | Expensive*

LONE STAR CAFÉ AND BAR
Massive portions in a country-and-western atmosphere. *14 Brecon St. | dinner daily | tel. 03 4 42 99 95 | Budget–Moderate*

MINAMI JUJISEI
Excellent Japanese cuisine. *45 Beach St. | dinner daily | tel. 03 4 42 98 54 | Moderate*

INSIDERTIP VESTA ☙
Take a seat, enjoy a cup of tea and gaze over the lake – preferably in the little greenhouse next to the old cottage, that has obviously survived the odd flood or two and in which lots of lovely designer articles are sold in spite of everything – jewellery, ceramics, furniture and accessoires, books, honey, stationery … *19 Marine Parade | www.vestadesign.co.nz*

SHOPPING

WINE TASTING
Here you can sample and buy everything made from grapes that grow so far in the south. Otago wines are not cheap, but rich and full-bodied. The rosés are also high quality. *14 Beach St./O'Connells Pavilion | tel. 03 4 09 22 26 | www.winetastes.com*

THE HOME OF BUNGEE

● On the South Sea island *South Pentecost* (Vanuatu), this near-death head-dive is an old ritual among young men. This was turned into the Bungee Jump in New Zealand – a success story that gained worldwide attention. The Kiwi adventurer A. J. Hackett made the first jump in mid 1989; carefully at first from a cablecar over soft snow, then illegally from the Eiffel Tower in Paris and ultimately from the historic Kawarau Bridge near Queenstown – always with a thick elastic rope and an ankle attachment. Bungee is a very lucrative tourist attraction down under. Adrenalin junkies from around the world pay a lot of money to hurl themselves into Nevis Valley 130m (425ft) below or from the top of Bob's Peak.

Just one of the many thrills in Queenstown: bungee jumping

LEISURE & SPORTS

'Action' is the keyword in Queenstown. The range of things on offer will make your head spin. The first bungee jump ever from the 43m (141ft)-high *Kawarau Suspension Bridge* on the SH 6 was a leap all the way to the bank for A. J. Hackett *(130 NZ$ per jump | tel. 03 4 42 71 00)*. Watching from the modern visitor centre is exciting too. And if this jump isn't daring enough, then you have a choice: the next grade includes the *Legde Bungy* ('only' 47m/154ft, but a heart-stopping 400m (1312ft) above Queenstown on Bob's Peak), the *Pipeline Bungy* in Skippers Canyon (102m/335ft) and Nevis Highwire (134m/440ft). Wild *white-water rafting tours,* that start 19km (12mi) away in Deep Creek (Shotover River), finish near Edith Cavall Bridge *(Arthurs Point Rd.),* at the waterfalls *(Queenstown Rafting | tel. 03 4 42 97 92 | www.rafting.co.nz)*. The *Shotover Jet,* the most thrilling jetboat trip of all *(tel. 0800 74 68 68 | www.shotover jet.com)*, also starts at the bridge. 'Combos' are a combination of several activities *(www.combos.co.nz)*. The ultimate thrill is the 'awesome foursome' which certainly gets the adrenalin going: Nevis bungee, a trip on the Shotover Jet, a helicopter trip to Skippers Canyon and then white-water rafting on Shotover River *(599 NZ$)*. River surfing on narrow boogy boards in thunderous waters, paragliding from Bob's Peak – only after a week at the earliest will you have time to relax! *Coronet Peak* is a first-class ski area in winter. All tours can be booked at *The Station | corner Camp/Shotover St. | tel. 03 442 7100 or 0800 28 64 95 | www. ajhackett.com.*

The rough mountain terrain makes mountainbikers' hearts beat faster. Try Skippers Canyon or head for Macetown. The leaflet *Mountainbike Riding* available through *www.gravityaction.com* or at the *Department of Conservation* DOC *(36 Shotover St. | www.doc.govt.nz)*, is useful when planning routes. Bikes can be hired in the same building *Outside Sports (tel. 03 4 41 00 47 | www.outsidesports.co.nz | 55 NZ$/day).*

ONSEN HOT POOLS ● ⛄

The exclusive spa with uninterrupted views of Kawarau gorge has six private pools heated to 38.6°C. Romantics pick the outdoor ones – by candlelight in the evening. *Daily 11am–11pm | 85 NZ$/hour for 2 | 160 Arthurs Point Rd. | 10 min. drive from Queenstown | free shuttle bus from the station in the centre | www.onsen. co.nz*

T.S.S. EARNSLAW (142 C3) *(ⓜ C15)*

This old steamship, with its clearly visible trail of smoke, chugs around Lake Wakatipu six times a day. The 2-hour trip takes in *Walter Peak Country Sheep and Cattle Station,* which holds demonstrations of

So bungee jumping is not enough? Then take a jetboat up Shotover River

life on an upland farm. *Real Journeys | Steamer Wharf | 50–70 NZ$ | tel. 03 442 75 00*

ENTERTAINMENT

Lively pubs include *Dux de lux (14 Church St., daily from 11pm), Lone Star Saloon (14 Brecon St.), Pog Mahone (Rees St.)* and *Speights Ale House (corner Stanley St./ Ballarat St.).*

WHERE TO STAY

Caravans and dormobiles are squeezed onto the local campsite *(Queenstown Lakeview Holiday Park | Brecon St. | tel. 03*

4 42 72 52 or 0800 48 27 35 | www.holiday park.net.nz | Budget). There's more room and natural surroundings on the shore at **INSIDER TIP** *Twelve Mile Delta Campsite*, managed by the DOC. No showers but running water and WCs *(Glenorchy Rd. | approx. 10km (6mi) north of Queenstown | Budget).*

COPTHORNE RESORT ⚜
Contemporary living and close to town with a view of the lake. *247 rooms | corner Aidelaide St./Frankton Rd. | tel. 03 442 8123 | www.copthornelakefront.co.nz | Moderate*

CROWNE PLAZA ⚜
Rooms in the front building have views over Lake Wakatipu. Just a short walk to the centre but quiet. *140 rooms | Beach St. | tel. 03 4 41 00 95 and 0800 18160 68 | www.ichotelsgroup.com | Expensive*

THE GLEBE
Flats perfect for small groups and self catering. *2 Beetham St. | tel. 03 4 41 03 10 | www.theglebe.co.nz | Moderate–Expensive*

THOMAS' BACKPACKERS
Cheap, centrally located accommodation with a restaurant. Right on the lake. *26 rooms | 50 Beach St. | tel. 03 4 42 71 80 | www.thomashotel.co.nz | Budget–Moderate*

INFORMATION

DEPARTMENT OF CONSERVATION (DOC)
Leaflets with hiking tours in the area. *36 Shotover St., 1st floor | tel. 03 4 42 79 35 | www.doc.govt.nz*

QUEENSTOWN I-SITE
Shotover St./Camp St. | tel. 03 4 42 4100. Information on cheap hotel accommo-

dation. *www.queenstown-nz.co.nz, www. queenstownadventure.com*

WHERE TO GO

ARROWTOWN (142 C3) (*ω C15*)

Once a gold mining town, founded in 1862, with beautifully restored wooden buildings housing lots of different souvenir shops. The *Chinese Settlement*, a sort of open-air museum that you reach after a gentle stroll along the banks of the Arrow River, tells of the destitute existence eked out by the vast majority of Chinese gold diggers *(signposted on Buckingham St.).* In mid April a colourful autumn festival is held when you can find out a lot about gold mining methods in *Lakes District Centennial Memorial Museum (Buckingham St. | daily 9am–5pm | 10 NZ$).* Scenes from 'Lord of the Rings' were filmed in the surrounding area on Arrow River. *20km (12½mi) north*

CLYDE (143 D3) (*ω C15*)

This little village is near the huge dam, 100m high and 500m long. Romantic **INSIDER TIP** *Oliver's Central Otago (Main St. | tel. 03 4 49 26 00 | www.oliverscentral otago.co.nz | Moderate)* in the converted stables and former general store complex is worth a visit. *95km (59mi) southeast*

CORONET PEAK (142 C3) (*ω C15*)

In summer, you can hike to the top (1646m/5400ft) in about an hour and enjoy the lovely view of Mt. Aspiring and Mt. Cardrona. In winter, it is a ski region. *15km (9½mi) north*

GLENORCHY (142 C3) (*ω C15*)

A good road (45 min. drive) takes you to the end of Lake Wakatipu and lonesome Mt. Aspiring National Park. *Dart River Safaris (tel. 0800 32 78 53 | www.dartriver. co.nz)* organise trips to locations in 'Lord of the Rings' (Isengart and Lothlórien)

in the wild and romantic area around Glenorchy. *Glenorchy Fur Products* work with and sell mainly opossum pelts *(corner Mull/Argyle St. | tel. 03 4 42 77 72 | www. glenorchyfur.co.nz).* Anyone wanting to escape from touristy Queenstown will enjoy *Glenorchy Campground,* which also has cabins, rooms and dormitories *(2 Oban St. | tel. 03 4 41 03 03 | Budget).* Information: *Department of Conservation | tel. 03 4 42 99 37. 50km (31mi) northwest.*

MT. ASPIRING NATIONAL PARK (142–143 C–D 1–2) (*ω B–C14*)

New Zealand's second largest national park, popular among climbers and hikers, extends from Haast Pass to Lake Wakatipu.

Mountains, plains, rivers: every hiker's dream come true in Mt. Aspiring National Park

The rivers in the mountains feed the lakes and Wanaka. At the foot of Mt. Aspiring (3027m/9931ft), at the ranger station *Makarora* (on the SH 6 between Wanaka and Haast Pass) the 🔅 *Siberia Experience* starts – a combined flight/hiking/jetboat tour (4 hours) through breathtaking mountain scenery *(mid Oct–mid April | Haast Pass Tourist Service | Makarora | approx. 270 NZ$ | tel. 03 4 43 86 66 | www.siberia experience.co.nz). 60km (37mi) north*

OTAGO GOLDFIELDS HERITAGE HIGHWAY
(143 D–E 3–4) (*ØØ C–D 15–16*)

The route takes in Cromwell, Alexandra, Roxburgh and Lawrence, from Alexandra also St Bathan's and Ranfurly, and leads to a number of old gold mines. The *Vulcan Hotel (tel. 03 4 47 36 29 | Moderate)* in *St Bathan's* (143 D3) (*ØØ D15)*, is run by 12 families and has 9 simply furnished rooms. A leaflet on the Heritage Highway *(www.goldfieldstrust.org.nz)* is available from the Department of Conservation in Queenstown. Further information under *www.maniototo.co.nz* and *www.central otagonz.com*

SKIPPERS CANYON 🔅
(142 C3) (*ØØ C15)*

This impressive canyon was an eldorado for gold-diggers in the mid 19th century. A few farming families and prospectors still live in the valley today. In places, the slopes are eroded and void of vegetation. Journeys in hire cars along the narrow and often dangerous roads are not covered by insurance. For guided tours on quad bikes contact *(Denis Columb | tel. 03 4 42 78 58 | www.offroad.co.nz). 10km (6mi) north*

WANAKA
(143 D2) (*∅ C14–15*)

The laid back answer to Queenstown. Wanaka promotes 'gentle tourism'. ● *Puzzling World* includes a 3-D maze, various 'Illusion Rooms' and a Puzzle Centre, perfect for that rainy day *(daily 8.30am–5pm | 2km (1¼mi) from Wanaka on the SH 84 | www.puzzlingworld.co.nz).* A paraglide flight over Lake Wanaka is quite an experience *(School of Paragliding | day course approx. 140 NZ$ | tel. 03 4 43 91 93).* Don't miss the *Aeroplane* and intriguing *Automobile and Transport Museum (daily 9am–5pm | 12 NZ$)* or the INSIDER TIP *Wanaka Beerworks*, one of New Zealand's best breweries, at the small airport. Every second (even) year, some 100,000 visitors come to the 'Warbirds over Wanaka' air show at Easter.

The quiet little town with some good restaurants and low-priced motels is a convenient starting point for ski tours to ⛷ *Treble Cone* and *Cardrona Skifield* with its cosy restaurant in *Cardrona Hotel* which dates from 1865 *(20 rooms | tel. 03 4 43 81 53 | Moderate),* near the road up to the ski area. Hwy 89 leads to Queenstown via ⛷ *Crown Range*. This route is tarmaced but is sometimes closed in winter and offers breathtaking views over Wakatipu Valley and Lake Hayes.

Information: *Department of Conservation | Ardmore St. | tel. 03 4 43 12 33; Wanaka i-SITE | The Log Cabin, Waterfront | tel. 03 4 43 12 33 | www.lakewanaka.co.nz. 10km (6¼mi) east*

STEWART ISLAND

(142 B–C6) (*∅ B17–18*) **Stewart Island lies at the end of the world. Te Punga o Te Waka a Maui, 'The Anchor Stone of Maui's Canoe' is the name of the island in Maori mythology, South Island being the canoe in which the demi-god Maui pulled the 'fish' – North Island – out of the water.**

And if James Cook had been right in 1770, then probably fewer people would feel sick on their way to Stewart Island, as the British seafarer believed the island was just a peninsula on South Island. But, as it is, catamarans have to struggle to cross one of the roughest stretches of water in the world – the 32km (20mi)-wide *Foveaux Strait*. Although the island does have sunny days, fog and rain are more common, on average on 255 days a year.

Stewart Island, 'New Zealand's best kept secret', has long since opened itself to tourism and day-trips are offered and give a first impression of the island. You can take a minibus and explore the 20km (12½mi) of roads and *Halfmoon Bay (Oban),* the only settlment on the island, stroll past the three fish factories, a pub, the particularly charming *Church Hill Café/ Restaurant (Kamahi Rd.),* the primary school, the little museum and the groceries that, through the lack of competition, is called a supermarket. Or relax for a few minutes on *Fred Lonnecker Beach*, a small section of the coastline that is 1600km (994mi) long. 200km (124mi) of trails lead over generally soft ground through dense forest and provide a closer look at this island that covers 650mi² and, in 2002, became New Zealand's 14th and most recent national park.

Fishermen often land good catches on Stewart Island: but good weather is less frequent

Ornithologists and botanists account for the majority of tourists to Stewart Island. If you're lucky, perhaps a shy kiwi will scamper past among the thick fern. In winter the average temperature is 9°C (48°F), in summer 18°C (64°F). But that is of little interest to nature-loving hikers or anglers who reel in flounder, salmon, tuna, cod, red snappers, scallops and crayfish from the Pacific and the nearby South Polar Ocean.

'Glowing Skies', is the Polynesian name for Stewart Island. The gravestone of the Wohlers, a husband and wife team of missionaries who lived together with the Maori on the island between 1844 and 1855, can be seen near *Ringaringa Beach*. *Ulva Island* in Paterson Inlet, with wonderful beaches, a fascinating bird life and a forest trail, can be reached by water taxi from Halfmoon Bay in 30 mins. *(www.ulva.co.nz)*.

SIGHTSEEING

PATERSON INLET

Trips to the ★ ● ⚡ *Observation Point* above Paterson Inlet are particularly romantic. On clear nights, the *Southern Cross* constellation can be seen easily – symbolically reproduced on the New Zealand flag as four stars forming a cross. *Rakiura*,

LEISURE & SPORTS

INSIDER TIP ▶ KIWI SPOTTING

Quietly follow the tracks of the plump kiwi at twilight *(Bravo Adventure Cruises | tel. 03 2 19 11 44 | www.kiwispotting.co.nz or Ruggedy Range | tel. 03 2 19 10 66 | www.ruggedyrange.com | book long in advance!)*.

STEWART ISLAND

NORTH WEST CIRCUIT

One of the most popular trails in the north of the island. The 125km (78mi)-long route takes 7–8 days. You must be in excellent physical shape and have sturdy, waterproof gear. The sparsely equipped cabins, set a day's walk apart, are free *(no reservations!)*. There are lots of hikers in Dec and Jan. An alternative is the 36km (22½mi)-long *Rakiura Track* which is well maintained with boardwalks. You need a *Great Walks Pass* from the Department of Conservation for the 3-day hike.

ENTERTAINMENT

Nightlife on Steward Island is limited to one surviving bar with a billiard table in *South Sea Hotel* on the harbour.

WHERE TO STAY

There are only a few motels such as the *South Sea Hotel (tel. 03 2 19 10 59 | www.stewart-Island.co.nz | Budget–Moderate)*. Ask at the i-SITE or see *www.stewartisland.co.nz*.

GETTING THERE

With the 'Foveaux Express' catamaran *(60 min. | from Bluff Sept–April daily e.g. 9.30am and 5pm, from Stewart Island 90 min. earlier | Stewart Island Marine | tel. 03 2 12 76 60 | www.stewartisland experience.co.nz | pedestrians only!)* or by air from Invercargill *(Stewart Island Flights | several times a day | tel. 03 2 18 91 29 | www.stewartislandflights.com | luggage max. 15 kg)*. Flights from 175 NZ$ (return), the ferry costs approx. 120 NZ$. The youth hostel in Invercargill organises cheap flights to the island (also on stand-by basis). For collectors of superlatives: the civil airport that is the furthest from the British Isles is on Stewart Island!

INFORMATION

DEPARTMENT OF CONSERVATION

Maps and leaflets on walks. *Main Road | tel. 03 2 19 00 02 | www.doc.govt.nz*

STEWART ISLAND VISITOR INFORMATION

12 Elgin Tce. | tel. 03 2 19 14 00 | www.stewartisland.co.nz

WHERE TO GO

BLUFF

(142 C5) *(ꝏ C17)*

This is home to a large fleet of fishing vessels and the site of a giant aluminium smelter. The ferry to Stewart Island from Bluff takes an hour. The southern-most point is where to can take your souvenir photo of the signpost showing the distance to various places such as New York 15,008km (9326mi) away. The South Pole is a mere 5200km (3230mi).

INVERCARGILL

(142 C5) *(ꝏ C17)*

The chilly damp town in the far south of South Island is short of attractions – but the few it has are not to be sneered at. The rare *tuatara*, the prehistoric-looking lizard can be marvelled at in its terrarium in *Southland Museum & Art Gallery,* where it 'freezes' but is actually very much alive *(Mon–Fri 9am–5pm, Sat/Sun from 10am | 108 Gala St. | tel. 03 2 18 97 53)*. In *Anderson Park Art Gallery,* housed in a colonial gentleman's house, art fans with a penchant for detail will not be able to get enough *(daily 10.30am–5pm | 91 McIvor Rd.)*. And should the sun actually come out, the usually deserted *Oreti Beach* soon heaves with people. *Victoria Railway Hotel* conceals modern creature comforts behind a 19th-century façade *(11 rooms | corner Leven/Esk St. | tel. 03 2 18 12 81 or 0800 77 75 57 |*

www.hotelinvercargill.com | *Moderate–Expensive).* Information: *Invercargill i-SITE* | *Gala St.* | *Southland Museum* | *tel. 03 2 14 62 43* | *www.southland.org.nz, www.invercargill.org.nz*

TE ANAU

(142 B3) *(𝔐 B15)* **This little town in the southeast corner of Lake Te Anau is the starting point for tours of Fiordland National Park. Covering 4650mi², it is New Zealand's largest park, only part of which has been explored.**

The first settlers also came across this rainforest which led to all sorts of creepy tales about the 'great hairy *moehau*', a pack of big-footed apes. Other blood-curdling horror stories are about the tiny but nasty sandflies whose bite still itches days later. Covering 135mi² Lake Te Anau is the largest lake on the whole of South Island with fjords reaching far inland.

Fiordland was created some 500 million years ago and has remained wild and inaccessible to this day. Doubtful Sound and especially Milford Sound are best equipped to deal with tourism. Those looking forward to a long hike in a pristine natural environment should be aware that up to 7m of rain is recorded in the Fiordland region annually. And some parts are pretty adventurous. Suspension bridges across rivers and gorges are sometimes little more than three wires, one for the feet and two for the hands.

SIGHTSEEING

GLOWWORM CAVES

'The Cave of Swirling Water' *(Te Ana-au)* is a unique cave full of glowworms only accessible by a 30-min. boat-trip from Te Anau. Glowworms are the larvae of a species of fly that attract other insects which they then eat. *Real Journeys* | *Te Anau* | *daily 2pm and 8.15pm* | *63 NZ$* | *tel. 03 2 49 74 16*

The tuatara: compared to this ancient reptile, *Homo sapiens* is a very young species

LEISURE & SPORTS

HIKING

This undisturbed wilderness is a paradise for hikers and nature-lovers. The ☆ *Milford Track* is the most popular hike – and well frequented. Guided tours are expensive but individual hikers also have to pay *(approx. 210 NZ$ incl. transfers, can be booked in advance by credit card)* and you must register weeks in advance in writing at the *Fiordland National Park Visitor Centre (tel. 03 2 49 85 14 | www.doc.govt.nz)*. The 54km (34mi)-long trail calls for a good level of fitness. You will be hiking 6 hours a day and the tour takes 4 days. The track passes through dream-like scenery, passing *Mirror Lakes* in which the mountains are reflected. It starts at Glade House (northern-most end of Lake Te Anau) and finishes in Milford *(guided tour: 5 days with accommodation in cabins, approx. 2000 NZ$ | www.ultimatehikes.co.nz)*. Alternatively try the ☆ *Routeburn Track* that can be done in 3 days (39km/24¼mi) which starts at Glenorchy (Lake Wakatipu) and ends 30km (18½mi) short of Milford Sound, passing through fascinating mountainous scenery on the way. The best time to hike is Nov–March *(Ultimate Hikes | www.ultimatehikes.co.nz)*. 1 day hikes also available *(approx. 175 NZ$)*.

WHERE TO STAY

FIORDLAND LODGE

Cosy lodge in log cabin style with a view of the lake and a small restaurant. *10 rooms | 472 Te Anau Milford Highway | 10 min. by car from Te Anau | tel. 03 2 49 78 32 | www. fiordlandlodge.co.nz | Expensive*

TOP 10 HOLIDAY PARK MOUNTAIN VIEW

Centrally located campsite on the shore road. Very popular, reservation advisable.

128 Te Anau Tce. | tel. 03 2 49 74 62 | www. teanautop10.co.nz | Budget

INFORMATION

FIORDLAND NATIONAL PARK VISITOR CENTRE

Information and reservation centre for hikes. *Lakefront Dr. | Te Anau | tel. 03 2 49 79 24 | www.doc.govt.nz*

TE ANAU I-SITE

Lakefront Dr. | tel. 03 2 49 89 00 | www. fiordlandnz.com

If you want to park your car safely while away hiking, book a place through *www. saferparking.co.nz (tel. 03 2 49 71 98 | campervan approx. 9 NZ$/day)* in Te Anau.

WHERE TO GO

INSIDER TIP ▶ DOUBTFUL SOUND ☆
(142 A3) *(ⓜ A15)*

This fantastic tour (just under 7 hours), takes you past *Lake Manapouri*, at 450m (1480ft) the deepest and for many the most beautiful lake in New Zealand, to Doubtful Sound. The electric power station on the west arm of the lake can be visited. Its gigantic turbine hall is 200m (656ft) below ground. Almost all energy generated is used by the aluminium smelter. Reservations: *Real Journeys | Lakefront Dr. | Te Anau | 280 NZ$ from Te Anau or Lake Manapouri | tel. 03 2 49 74 16 | www.realjourneys.co.nz*

MILFORD SOUND ★ ☆
(142 B2) *(ⓜ B14–15)*

The 1692m (5551)-high *Mitre Peak* is the best-known photo motif in Milford Sound. Boat tours lasting around 1½ hours ply the 16km (10mi)-long fjord down to the Tasman Sea, passing the huge Bowen Falls, colonies of seals and penguins, and accompanied by dolphins. A view below the water is also worth it: the *Underwater Observatory Milford Deep* in *Harrison Cove* takes you 8m down into the realm of the red coral and seahorse and gives an impressive picture of the darker reaches of the fjord. *Red Boat Cruises*, *Mitre Peak Cruises* and *Real Journeys* include this in some of their Milford Sound tours. The tours between 11am and 2.30pm are especially popular.

For those in a hurry, try the Coach 'n' Fly day-trip *(Real Journeys | Steamer Wharf | Queenstown | approx. 590 NZ$ | tel. 03 4 42 75 00)* from Queenstown: by bus to Milford Sound, then a boat-trip up the Sound and back to Queenstown by plane. The return trip by plane from Queenstown is also popular *(duration of trip: 4 hours, incl. 90 min. boat-trip on the Sound | Air Milford | 430 NZ$ | tel. 0800 46 22 52 |*

Milford Sound: amazingly beautiful both above and below the water

The car journey from Te Anau to Milford (100km/62mi) takes about 2½ hours. This is arguably the most beautiful mountain road in New Zealand passing *Mirror Lakes* and the dark 1.2km (¾mi)-long *Homer Tunnel* beyond which the weather often changes abruptly. Virtually all tourists stop here to feed the cheeky but likeable alpine parrots, the keas. A bad habit that doesn't do the birds any good.

www.airmilford.co.nz). ● **INSIDER TIP** Cabin cruisers also ply the fjord: 'Milford Wanderer' *(405 NZ$ from Te Anau)*, and 'Milford Mariner' *(approx. 500 NZ$ from Te Anau | reservations under www.real journeys.co.nz)*. Apart from a basic backpacker lodge with campervan pitches *(Milford Sound Lodge | tel. 03 2 49 80 71)* there is nowhere else to stay on Milford Sound.

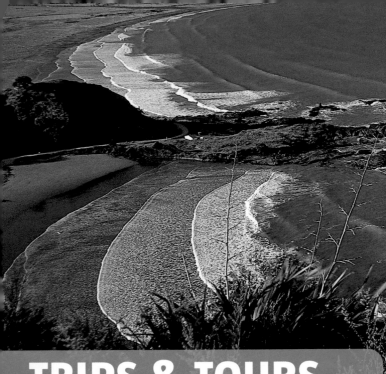

TRIPS & TOURS

The tours are marked in green in the road atlas, the pull-out map and on the back cover

1 EASTLAND – NEW ZEALAND'S WILD EASTERN REGION

Dark beaches along the western side strewn with driftwood; golden, soft sandy bays in the east and, in between, the cliffs at East Cape pertly jutting into the Pacific. The Pacific Coast Highway passes through one of the most remote corners of North Island, inhabited largely by Maori in little villages. This is also where the wine-growing town of Gisborne is – 'The First City To See The Light'. The route from Opotiki to Gisborne takes 2–3 days (334km/208mi).

An endless string of dunes and beaches just beyond Opotiki. The terraced slopes at Tirohanga Bluff are testimony to an early Maori settlement. Everytime the Pacific Coast Highway turns back to the coast after winding its way through the steep hinterland, you will be welcomed by the thundering sound of the waves. The wild water of the Motu River above the estuary is ideal for thrilling rafting trips starting from Opotiki. Comfortable places to stay along the route include ☆ Te Kaha Hotel (tel. 07 3 25 28 30 | www. tekahabeachresort.co.nz) with 14 simply furnished rooms and breathtaking sea-views, and Pacific Coast Macademias

Photo: East Cape

Along the coast road through the wild eastern region of North Island or with the kajak in rainforest lagoons past colonies of seals

(*Whanarua Bay | www.macanuts.co.nz*), where the nuts are grown and sold. Tourists are treated brusquely but sincerely in Eastland as long as they keep off Maori land marked 'Private Property'. Fine sandy Whangaparaoa Bay below the steeply rising Cape Runaway is tribal country from which 'neither sand nor stones may be removed'. Pass the sleepy Maori settlement Te Araroa and probably the oldest

pohutukawa tree, around 600 years old, the route leads to the eastern-most point in New Zealand. High up at East Cape a brilliant white lighthouse warns ships of dangerous rocks.

The Pacific Coast Highway twists and turns through the densely forested mountains. Where the valleys open up to form a wide expanse of farmland there is a collection of plain houses that make up Ruatoria, the centre of the warlike Maori of the Ngati Porou tribe. They own **Mt. Hikurangi** (1754m/5755ft) that can only be climbed with permission if you want to witness the first sunrays of the new day across the Pacific.

When sunbathing on wonderful **Wainui Beach** it's difficult to imagine that whales repeatedly get stranded here and perish. The fenced sandy hillock nearby is a mass grave for the 59 sperm whales that died in 1970 alone. The award-winning box-hit

Even the first settlers planted vines in the Gisborne area

Further south, the coastline slowly loses its ruggedness until one sandy bay follows the next. **Waipiro Bay**, kept alive by a *marae* is worth a detour as is **Wharekaka Bay** which is steeped in important events in Maori mythology. Take a warm bath en route in the geothermal waters at INSIDER TIP *Te Puia Springs* (in the hotel / *tel. 06 864 6755*) before turning off to **Tokomaru Bay** and its long jetty. If you don't skip **Tolaga Bay** you can enjoy a 2.6km (1½mi) walk along INSIDER TIP *Cooks Cove Walkway* to the picturesque caves.

'Whale Rider' made in 2002 was filmed in the village **Whangara**. Guided tours with *Trevor Brown (Ngatapa / tel. 06 868 6139 / incl. Farmstay)*. **Poverty Bay** brings you to the friendly coastal town of **Gisborne**, the heart of a small but very good wine-growing region. The i-SITE in the centre has leaflets on the wineries *(209 Grey St. / tel. 06 868 6139 / www.gisbornenz.com)*. To the west of Gisborne the Pacific Coast Highway connects with Hwy 2 that will take you back to where you started this tour. Information: *www.pacificcoast.co.nz*

2 PADDLING PAST THE RAINFOREST

The most sporty and original way to get to know the fascinating coastline of Abel Tasman National Park is definitely by kajak. This tour takes you past the park's picturesque sandy bays. While hikers have to cope with hordes of others on the crowded coastal track, you can enjoy the gentle breeze on the water and head for deserted beaches for your picnic. So that you actually find these and other beautiful corners, and don't have to do without a sociable evening around a campfire, we recommend the guided 3-day 'Classic Tour' from Marahau Beach. Tents, kajaks and food is provided. Sleeping bags and food are charged for separately *(Abel Tasman Kayaks | tel. 03 5 27 80 22 or 0800 52 78 02 | www. abeltasmankayaks.co.nz | from 615 NZ$)*. 1-day trips are also available.

Tents, sleeping bags, food and other equipment are stowed in the watertight hatch. Life jackets and spray skirts are put on first and the foot controls tested. After a few dry runs for inexperienced paddlers – it's off you go. On **Marahau Beach** at the southern end of the national park, 4 kajaks take to the water: 3 2-seaters for participants and 1 1-seater for the guide. Final instructions are given and then you paddle off into the gentle waves of Sandy Bay. The first stop is in **Akersten Bay** where the group has to prepare its own lunch on the beach. Protected by **Adele Island** even novices can practice how to use the paddle and to steer. A colony of seals has taken up home on the island. **Appletree Bay** and **Stilwell Bay** are the names of pretty crescents of sand that you reach after around 3 hours. With a bit of luck you may be accompanied by playful delphins that suddenly appear and bob up and down alongside the kajaks. The lunch break gives you time for a swim or a short walk in the shade of the forest. Once back on the water, you now face your first real challenge: the waves whipped up by the wind around the rocky coast of **Pitts Head**. Round the corner the calm water flows past **Torrent Bay** and its tiny islets. Depending on the tide, you may be able enter a huge lagoon surrounded by thick forest which provides an ideal habitat for both sea and forest birds. The kajaks glide out again with the tide and battle against the prevalent northerly wind to **North Head** where you camp for the night. The group will certainly be on its own here as the busy hiking trail is around 1km (½mi) further inland. Dinner will be surprisingly tasty and even a bottle of wine will be produced.

Tonga Island, further north, is where you'll be heading for on the second day passing one magically beautiful bay after another on the way, but you can only get into **Frenchman Bay** and **Sandfly Bay** at high tide. You can tell the track runs along the water again by the hikers on the beach at Sandfly Bay, as well as in the next one, **Bark Bay**, which are inviting places to swim. But often time is too short and Tonga Island is still some way away. The island is part of a marine reserve where fishing is prohibited. Up to 200 seals live on Tonga Island. The young in particular are trusting and their inquisitiveness brings them close to the kajaks. The second day finishes in the afternoon on the beach at **Tonga Quarry**, giving you enough time to swim, snorkel and hike. You can take an invigorating shower under a nearby waterfall which is easily reached on foot. If you go on the night-time paddle trip – which is especially romantic under clear skies and with a full moon – will get to bed pretty late. The start the next day on the last leg is therefore a little later.

In the morning the northerly breeze helps blow you back home. All the kajaks are used to make a raft and the strong wind from behind is caught in the sail hoisted between two paddles. A detour to Sandfly Bay at high tide leads through the estuary of the Falls River up as far as a frightingly narrow suspension bridge that, high above your head, links the two forested banks. The stronger the wind blows, the faster the kajak raft is blown towards Marahau. Perhaps there will still be time for a last stop at Adele Island. Unfortunately it's too early for the delightful blue penguins that seek out their nests here later in the evening.

3 ROMANTIC CYCLE TOUR THROUGH OTAGO

Away from main roads, this tour will take you into the thinly populated upland area of Central Otago – called 'Big Sky Country' – as the sky stretches like a huge blue arch over endless chains of hills. Dreamy little villages uphold the memory of a glorious past, long since faded, when in the 19th century gold caused a boom in this remote part. Even the railway that used to run along the coast was abandoned sometime. What was retained is now used by the *Taieri Gorge Railway* for spectacular excursions into the rocky gorge. The remaining 150km (90mi) is a well-prepared railway line minus the tracks that has been opened as the *Otago Central Rail Trail*, a traffic-free stretch exclusively for walkers, cyclists and riders *(www.otagorailtrail.co.nz)*. From Dunedin, take the Taieri Gorge Railway to Pukerangi or Middelmarch, then cycle for 3–5 days (depending on how fit you are) to Clyde. You can also arrange your own organised trip incl. rental bike, luggage forwarding and

accommodation *(e-tours recreational cycling | 67 Stuart St. | Dunedin | tel. 03 4 71 84 38 | www.cyclesurgery.co.nz)*.
The nostalgic trips starts at the railway station in Dunedin. Railway fans and those who prefer fresh air are best advised to sit by the sliding windows in the old heritage carriages from the 1920s rather than in the air-conditioned panorama carriages. Bicycles are transported free of charge. Slowing down a bit, the train soon reaches the unspoilt mountain scenery. Unremittingly you carry on up through narrow tunnels and across spindly bridges. After 2½ hours the train halts at Pukerangi. Only in summer on Friday and Saturday does the journey continue to Middlemarch which connects up with the Otago Central Rail Trail just 200m from the station. If you alight in Pukerangi, you must either take a bus to Middlemarch or cycle the 19km (12mi) along the main road.
At Hyde you follow part of the old line past rusty waggons and derelict station buildings. It isn't until you reach Ranfurly that you'll have the charm and comfort of a little town. The self-proclaimed Art Deco oasis has gained a certain modest fame due to the annual *Art Deco Weekend* held in February – all thanks to the enterprising Edna McAtamney, who sells genuine articles from the period in her shop Decollectables on the main road and provides a bed for the night in Moyola Guest House, furnished with period pieces *(3 rooms, each 150 NZ$ incl. breakfast | 250 NZ$ for all three | 38 Charlemont St. | tel. 03 4 44 90 10 or 0800 99 99 79 | edna@nzsouth.co.nz)*. Even the old railway buildings have been spruced up nicely and house a tiny local radio station. The highest point of the Rail Trail is marked at Wedderburn: 618m (2028ft). Just beyond this you cross the latitude 45° South. In the idyllic village of Oturehua

there is an unspoilt general store more than 100 years old. Simple but comfortable accommodatioin can be found in the village at **Poolburn Hotel** *(8 rooms | Ida Valley Rd. | tel. 03 4 47 47 75 | Budget)*. **Broadhaven**, 20km (12½mi) further on in Lauder, is an old schoolhouse that has been converted into a charming B&B *(dinner available | 5 rooms | tel. 03 4 47 30 99 | broadhaven@xtra.co.nz | Budget)*.

from the goldrush era – is well worth it. **Alexandra** is an inviting place for a break, as the little town – blessed with a Mediterranean climate – has a number of good restaurants *(e.g. Briar & Thyme | tel. 03 4 48 91 89 | Budget–Moderate)* and excellent wine estates *(e.g. Dry Gully | tel. 03 4 49 20 59 or Hawkdun Rise Vineyard with B&B | 2 rooms | 241 Letts Gully Rd. | tel. 03 4 48 77 82 | www.vineyardstay.co.nz | Moderate)*.

Dunedin's historic station and Taieri Gorge Railway mark the start of the cycle tour

Beyond **Auripo** the more rugged mountain scenery starts and with it, the most interesting section of the trail: high viaducts and long tunnels (don't forget a torch!). After the bridge over the Manuherikia River you return to gentle farmland. In Omakau, the 2km (1¼mi) detour to **Ophir** – a picturesque settlement dating

Clyde marks the end of the Rail Trail. This charming place, full of memories of golden riches, has a remarkable **Railway Museum** in the old station buildings. Cosy rooms can be found in the historic **Dunstan Hotel** *(15 rooms | 35 Sunderland St. | tel. 03/4 49 28 17 | www.dunstanhotel. co.nz | Budget)*.

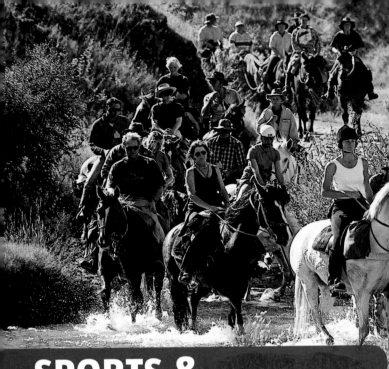

SPORTS & ACTIVITIES

With so many things on offer, even couch potatoes can't avoid doing something physically active. They can try a round on one of the beautiful golf courses, tackle a sweat-inducing mountainbike tour, a tandem paraglide or a bungee jump. Here are a few suggestions.

take an early morning trip on *Lake Wakatipu* with *Stu Dever (tel. 03 4 42 63 71)* where the chance is pretty good of hooking a fat rainbow trout. Sea-angling is good in the Bay of Islands. On *Geoff Stone's* boat *(tel. 027 4 37 78 44 | www.majortom.co.nz)* you can reel out the line for a swordfish.

FISHING

You can buy the necessary licences locally in most sports shops *(approx. 23 NZ$/day, 113 NZ$/season | www.fishandgame.org.nz)*, where you can also find out what the maximum day's catch is. Lake Taupo is famous for trout. If you are in Queenstown

GOLF

This popular sport in New Zealand is also an inexpensive treat for tourists *(green fee 20–45 NZ$/person, approx. 140 NZ$ on exclusive courses such as Millbrook near Arrowtown)*. The most attractive of the 400 golf courses include **INSIDER TIP** ▶

Photo: Riders crossing the Arrow River

The most exciting sportsground in the world: New Zealand has everything for nature freaks, water rats and adventurers

Kelvin Heights Golf Course on the peninsula in Lake Wakatipu near Queenstown *(Peninsula Rd. | Kelvin Heights | tel. 03 4 42 91 69)*, *Arikikapakapa Course* in Rotorua *(near the Maori Arts and Crafts Institute | tel. 07 3 48 40 51)* set among geothermal springs, the course at a *Waitangi* above the Bay of Islands with its view *(Tau Henere Dr. | tel. 09 4 02 77 13)* and the course in *Paraparaumu* near Wellington *(376 Kapiti Rd. | tel. 04 9 02 82 00)* surrounded by sand dunes.

HIKING

Detailed hiking maps and essential information such as the weather forecast are available locally from the *Departement of Conservation (DOC | www.doc.govt.nz)*. This is also where you can register for the most popular hikes that take several days: the 'Great Walks', e.g. the *Abel Tasman Coastal Track*, the *Lake Waikaremoana Track*, the *Milford Track* and the *Routeburn Track*. Sometimes it can get a bit cramped in the cabins along the hiking routes – it's better to take a tent and water with you. The *Te Araroa – The Long Pathway*, completed in 2011 – a 3000km (1865mi)-long route that links existing paths between Cape Reinga in the north and Bluff on the southern tip of South Island – is a real hiking marathon that takes you past volcanoes and over mountain passes, along the coast and rivers and through 7 towns *(www.teararoa.org.nz)*.

KAJAK & CANOE TRIPS

The Whanganui River will take you into the uninhabited wilderness of *Whanganui National Park*. Tours with rented canoes starting in Owhango are run by *Wades Landing Outdoors (tel. 06 8955995)*. *Abel Tasman Kayaks (tel. 03 5278022)* will take you from Marahau Beach to the lovely bays in *Abel Tasman National Park (p. 108)*. The idyllic solitude of the *Dart River* near *Glenorchy* can be experienced in inflatable canoes – 'fun yaks' *(tel. 03 4427374 | bus transfer from Queenstown)*.

MOUNTAINBIKING & CYCLING

Due to the growing number of cyclists, an initiative jointly financed by government funding, has started to create an attractive network of cycle paths throughout the country called *Nga Haerenga (tourism.govt. nz/OurWork/New-Zealand-Cycle-Trail-Project)*, aimed at making cycling in New Zealand more attractive for everybody. *NZ Pedaltours* in Auckland *(tel. 09 3020968)* arranges bus trips over several days when you only cycle the most attractive sections.

Guided cycling tours lasting several days are available starting in Christchurch: *Pacific Cycle Tours (tel. 03 3299913 | www.bike-nz.com)*. South Island has challenging mountainbike routes, e.g. individual tours for experienced bikers along the **INSIDER TIP** *Queen Charlotte Track* through the Marlborough Sounds *(March–Nov, Marlborough Sounds Adventure Company | tel. 03 5736078)* or guided tours through the gold-diggers' Skipper's Gorge near Queenstown *(Gravity Action | reservation through Information & Track Centre | 37 Shotover St. | tel. 03 4429708 | www.info track.co.nz)*. The *Otago Central Rail Trail (p. 110)* between Dunedin/Middlemarch and Clyde or Queenstown is particularly beautiful and well maintained. Information and reservations under *www.otago railtrail.co.nz*. Note: cyclists must wear helmets in New Zealand.

RIDING

Guides at *Backcountry Saddle Expedition* in Cardrona Valley between Wanaka and Queenstown with a good knowledge of the area and of horses take you on hacks (also for beginners) across the Southern Alps *(on Hwy 83 | tel. 03 4438151)*. Guided rides along the brilliant white sand on *Wharariki Beach* in Golden Bay *(Cape Farewell Horse Treks | tel. 03 5248031)* are also suitable for beginners.

RUNNING/JOGGING

A pair of running shoes in your luggage is perfect in New Zealand – as this is a nation always on the move – whether its along the beach early in the morning or around a park in the lunch break or after work – with junior pushed along in a special pram. And if jogging is not enough for you, you can always take part in one of the many running competitions. 'The more extreme, the more popular' seems to hold true *(www.coolrunning.co.nz, www.runningcalendar.co.nz).*

SAILING

The best area for sailing is without doubt the *Bay of Islands* with its strong winds and many sheltered bays. The route between Auckland and the Bay of Islands is also popular. See: *www.charterguide.co.nz* And if you only want to spend one day on the water, hoist the sail on *Lake Taupo.* The harbour in Taupo, where yachts wait for customers, is the place to start.

and foremost is the fully fledged ski arena *Coronet Peak* near Queenstown, and *The Remarkables* and *Cardrona* which have runs for experienced skiers too. The winter scenery around *Treble Cone* to the west of Wanaka is breathtaking. Information under *www.nzski.com, www.lakewanaka.co.nz, www.whakapapa.co.nz, www.snow.co.nz*

SURFING & WINDSURFING

The coastline of South Island seems to have been made for surfboards or the more compact boogie boards; windsurfing is better on North Island: e.g. off

Wonderful cycling tours can be had all over the place – and don't forget: 'Keep Left'

SKIING

Whoever finds themselves in New Zealand in winter (July–Sept) should head for the slopes and toboggan runs in *Ruapehu*, the only commercial winter sports area on North Island.

The *Waiorau Nordic Ski Area (www.snowfarmnz.com)* near Wanaka on South Island, not only has the only cross-country tracks in the country but it is also the most beautiful ski region in the Southern Alps. First

Oakura near New Plymouth, on *Piha Beach* to the west of Auckland and on *Orewa Beach* on the Hibiscus Coast. On South Island, *Sumner* near Christchurch suits most surfers. The shallow bay at *Ferrymead* is perfect for kite surfing especially (courses and rental: *East Coast Boardriding Co. Ltd. | 1091 Ferry Rd. | tel. 03 3 84 37 88).* The young surfing crowd congregate in *Raglan* on the west of North Island (courses/rental: *Raglan Surfing School | tel. 07 8 25 78 73 | www.raglan.net.nz).*

TRAVEL WITH KIDS

The birth rate in New Zealand is slightly higher than in the UK with an average of 2 children per family. For the Maori, children traditionally play a vital role as, long before the arrival of the Euopeans, offspring ensured the continued existence of the tribe.

Virtually every restaurant has high chairs and children's menus. Family restaurants keep the young ones occupied with drawing materials and a play area. And 'no worries' – nobody at the next table is going to glare at you just because your child is driving the noise level to new heights. Nappy-changing facilities can usually be found wherever there is a 'Ladies'.

Warming up a bottle is happily done by restaurant staff everywhere.

Little Kiwis are mad about ice cream which can be found on every corner, in every flavour and colour, and preferably really creamy. Top of the hotlist are the 180 different varieties at *Gourmet Ice Cream Co. (2 Awatea St. | Dunedin), Kapiti Ice Cream (Lindale Farm on the SH 1 in Paraparaumu between Levin and Wellington)* and *Rush Munro's Ice Cream*, that has long attracted generations of children after school into *Rush Munro's Ice Cream Garden (Heretaunga St. West, Hastings near Napier)*. Finding somewhere to stay with children does not have to be expensive. In many

Fun and games in Kiwi land: after that long-haul flight families find themselves in a particularly child-friendly country

hotel and motel rooms there are extra beds for little or no charge. And microwaves are not a rarity. Campsites often have cabins or bungalows to rent with a number of beds. If you hire a campervan, they can often sleep up to six. Children under 2 must travel in child seats; up to 5 years special safety harnesses are obligatory. Check with your car hire company in advance which will advise you.

Levels of hygiene and medical care are comparable to those in the UK. Hotels and motels fence in their pools. And anyone on a bike, whether big or small, has to wear a helmet.

On the other side of the world, more than anywhere else, care should be taken to protect a child's skin from the intensive rays of the sun. Special swimming costumes are available everywhere that deflect UV rays. At least crossing the road is no problem for British children: 'look right, look left, look right again' applies here too.

AUCKLAND ZOO (136 B1–2) *(ɯ H–J5)*
Spacious, state-of-the art, well-looked-after enclosures ensure animal encounters of the pleasant kind in the west of the city. And if the little ones are a bit wary of the tigers, lions or other predators, and know elephants, monkey and llamas from zoos at home, then show them the docile New Zealand animals in the next pens: little tuataras that look like living dinos, or kiwis that can only be seen in their darkened enclosure if you keep your eyes wide open and don't say a word – admittedly a test of patience even for adults that you will definitely never forget. *Daily 9.30am–5.30pm | Western Springs | Motions Rd. | adults 22 NZ$, children 11 NZ$ | www.aucklandzoo.co.nz*

HOT WATER BEACH (136 C1–2) *(ɯ K5)*
Fun guaranteed: dig holes in the sand as deep as you like and to your heart's content until the hot water from the natural geothermal springs comes up through the sand. Find out about the tides, as the springs are only accessible at low tide. Swimming in the sea can be dangerous and can only be recommended for strong swimmers due to the powerful currents. *South of Hahei on the eastern side of Coromandel Peninsula | tidal information: Whitianga Visitor Centre | tel. 07 8 66 55 55 | www.whitianga.co.nz*

KELLY TARLTON'S UNDERWATER WORLD & ANTARCTIC ENCOUNTER ●
(136 B1–2) *(ɯ H–J5)*
Thanks to the transparent acryllic tunnel, children can dive into the undersea world of the South Pacific without getting wet and without the sharks and manta rays circling above their heads doing them any harm. Next door, fascinating facts about the South Pole are explained in hands-on, interactive displays with, for example, real penguins that can be watched in their element. The Antarctic undersea world is also shown. *Daily 9am–6pm, in summer 9pm | Orakei Wharf, Tamaki Drive | Auckland | adults 34 NZ$, children 17 NZ$ | www.kellytarltons.co.nz*

SPLASH PLANET
(137 D6) *(ɯ K8)*
Following a thorough revamp this water park is really a fun place, especially on hot summer days which are quite frequent in *Hawke Bay*. Your children have the choice of indoor or outdoor pools, slides, a pirates' fort with spring boards, a children's railway, mini golf, beach volleyball, etc., etc., etc. *Summer daily 10am–6pm, winter Sat/Sun and public holidays 10am–5pm | 2km/1¼mi away in Windsor Park | Grove Rd. | Hastings | 30 NZ$ | www.splashplanet.co.nz*

VOLCANIC ACTIVITY CENTRE
(136 C4) *(ɯ K7)*
Being surrounded by so many spluttering craters, sizzling springs and hot steam as in the middle of North Island, it's good to explain to the children what all this volcanic activity is about. Difficult? 'No worries'. Together with your children you will enjoy the innovative audiovisual effects and learn masses about earthquakes and volcanism. *Mon–Fri 8.30am–5pm | Wairakei Park Taupo | entrance fee 11 NZ$*

INSIDER TIP ▸ WAIHEKE ISLAND
(136 B1) *(ɯ J5)*
A trip to this island in the Hauraki Gulf with its wonderful beaches is certainly going to add variety to your sightseeing tour. Whether at Oneroa, Palm Beach or

Railway trips from yesteryear are a holiday experience not to be forgotten

Onetangi, children have fun on the sand and in the water wherever they are. It can get a bit crowded here on sunny weekends when the Aucklanders hop across to the island in hordes. The ferry takes 35 mins. from Ferry Building *(Fullers Cruise Centre | Quay St. | tel. 09 3 67 91 11 | www. fullers.co.nz)*. Hire cars are at *Matiata Wharf (tel. 09 3 72 86 35)*. Information: *www.tourismwaiheke.co.nz*

SOUTH ISLAND

INSIDER TIP ► ANTIGUA BOAT SHEDS
(141 D5) *(ↂ F13)*

Family-sized rowing boats can be hired at the black-and-white boat sheds in which you can ferry your children through Christchurch's Botanical Garden. There is also a café. *Daily 10am–4.30pm | 2 Cambridge Terrace | Christchurch*

THE LUGE
(142 C3) *(ↂ C15)*

Bob's Peak doesn't just offer fantastic views for the parents but thrills for up-and-coming Formula One pilots: children over 10 can race down the hillside at the Skyline Luge on speedy sleds. *Daily 10am–dusk | Queenstown | 10 NZ$ a ride | www. skyline.co.nz*

THE PUZZLING WORLD
(143 D2) *(ↂ C14–15)*

Outside, children will need a little time to find their way out of the maze again. Inside, they will be astonished by the mass of weird illusions that seem to make the world stand on its head. All sorts of puzzles ensure that nobody gets bored on a rainy day. *Daily 8.30am–5pm | Hwy 6 | Wanaka | entrance fee 15.50 NZ$ | www. puzzlingworld.co.nz*

FESTIVALS & EVENTS

Not a nation for missing out on the fun, if a public holiday falls on a Sunday, it's moved to the following Monday. And Kiwis know how to party until they drop – and they have enough opportunities too: whether in the sports club, at charity or school events, at a barbecue or potluck dinner when each guest brings something for the buffet. At *Labour Weekend* in spring at the latest, the party will be outside. And then there's really nothing more to keep a New Zealander inside!

PUBLIC HOLIDAYS

1 January *New Year*; **6 February** *Waitangi Day*; **March/April** *Good Friday*, Easter Monday, **25 April** *ANZAC Day:* Remembrance Day; **1st Monday in June** *Queen's Birthday*; **4th Monday in October** *Labour Weekend*; **25 December** *Christmas Day*; **26 December** *Boxing Day*

For detailed information see: *www.tapeka.com/publicholidays.htm*

FESTIVALS & EVENTS

JANUARY

▶ *Buskers Festival:* 10-day free street performances in Christchurch by artists from around the world *(www.worldbuskers festival.com)*.
▶ *Glenorchy Races:* At horse races and rodeos set against a breath-takingly beautiful backdrop of mountains at the far end of Lake Wakatipu, the local farmers haven't been the sole spectators for some time now. Hearty festival fun. Bring your own picnic (1st weekend in Jan).

FEBRUARY

▶ *Speights Coast to Coast Triathlon:* 238km (148mi) across South Island: running, cycling, kajaking. Finish in Christchurch with a beach party in Sumner (mid Feb).
▶ *Marlborough Wine and Food Festival:* The oldest of the many culinary festivals and still one of the best and most popular. The number of visitors however is limited to 12,000. Book early to avoid disappointment. Tickets: *tel. 03 5 77 89 77* (end Feb).
▶ **INSIDER TIP** *Art Deco Festival:* 3rd weekend. Colourful street party in Napier with

Sheep-shearing and worm-eating: the New Zealanders like celebrating outside – with picnics and a bit of eccentricity thrown in

lots of music and fantastic costumes all in the spirit of the 'Roaring Twenties'.

MARCH

▶ INSIDER TIP *Wildfood Festival:* Thousands descend on Hokitika on the 2nd weekend to try the wine and food at this annual fair. And the 'Wild Coast' lives up to its name when 'everything wild', incl. worms, ends up on the barbeque.

▶ *Championship Golden Shears:* 400 sheep-shearers battle it out in Masterton at the beginning of the month.

▶ *New Zealand International Festival of Arts:* 3 weeks of top-notch culture (theatre, music, dance) held every 2nd year in Wellington.

▶ *WOMAD:* World of Music, Arts & Dance. The extensive park Brooklands in New Plymouth is turned over to artists one weekend long *(www.womad.co.nz and www.womad.org).*

APRIL

▶ *Arrowtown Autumn Festival:* When the leaves start to turn, the gold-digger town near Queensland is shown in all its glory. The highlight is the historical procession.

JUNE/JULY

▶ *Winter Festival:* Trick ski shows, classical concerts in the snow and ice sculptures mark the opening of the ski season in Queenstown.

▶ *Matariki:* Maori harvest festival and New Year's celebration with lots of different events. *(www.matarikifestival.org.nz)*

NOVEMBER

▶ INSIDER TIP *Rhododendron Festival:* For 2 weeks, more than 100 gardens in and around New Plymouth show off their blooms. *Pukeiti Rhododendron Garden (2290 Carrington Rd. | 20km (12½mi south-west)* is a must.

LINKS, BLOGS, APPS & MORE

LINKS

▶ www.muzic.net.nz Live performances, stars and chart hits – if you're interested in the New Zealand music scene, this is the site for you

▶ www.360newzealand.co.nz View a selection of high-quality 360° virtual tours to inspire your visit down under

▶ www.teara.govt.nz New Zealand's digital encyclopedia that is being developed, slowly but surely. If you're interested in history, then check out *www.nzhistory.net.nz*

▶ www.stuff.co.nz Up-to-the-minute news from across New Zealand

▶ www.organicexplorer.com The ecologically minded will find what they want here as well as all things organic around the country

▶ www.newzealand.com/int/map Everything you need to plan your trip around New Zealand. The interactive New Zealand map covers all key regions, towns, roads, national parks, rivers and lakes. Includes articles written by local experts and others

BLOGS & FORUMS

▶ www.nzvillage.com For the ex-pat community and visitors to New Zealand, Australia and the South Seas. Diverse blogs with many practical tips

▶ www.travelblog.org/Oceania/New-Zealand Blogging their hearts out at the other end of the world. More than 1000 blogs on both North and South Island, every region, town and in a variety of languages

▶ www.blognewzealand.co.uk Interesting, well-written blogs for both those living or travelling around New Zealand

Regardless of whether you are still preparing your trip or already in New Zealand: these addresses will provide you with more information, videos and networks to make your holiday even more enjoyable

▶ www.tvnz.co.nz New Zealand TV website with lots of films giving up-to-date information about what is going on in New Zealand

▶ www.radionz.co.nz/podcasts Huge selection of podcasts from Radio New Zealand on every conceivable topic to do with Kiwi country

▶ vimeo.com/21073193 A video for adrenalin freaks: breath-stopping tours by professional downhill-bikers through fantastic countryside around Queenstown – and all this by sunshine with cool music and cool bikers

▶ New Zealand Maps Once you have installed the free Outdoor Atlas app you can access detailed maps of New Zealand on your Smartphone, even offline, with this app extension

▶ Stuff.co.nz This free app from the online magazine *Stuff,* that was awared a prize in 2011 as New Zealand's best news medium, keeps you informed about politics, the economy, technology, sport, lifestyle and travel

▶ New Zealand Adrenaline Adventure Travel Looking for that ultimate thrill? Then this app is for you. Whether bungee jumping, sport climbing or rafting – every adventurer will find something exciting here

▶ www.tripbod.com Get to know the locals who are happy to act as 'live guides' for a small fee

▶ www.digsville.com Interested in house swapping? Then this is where to look. The simpler version *www.couchsurfing.com,* a worldwide network for cultural exchanges, etc. is an alternative. Tourists can connect up with people living in New Zealand

▶ www.facebook.com/purenewzealand The Facebook page of *New Zealand 100% Pure*, Tourism New Zealand, with tips, photos and information

TRAVEL TIPS

✈ To fly to the other side of the world you either take the west route (USA) or east (Asia). For flights with a stopover in America check security regulations and visa formalities beforehand. From the UK, several major airlines incl. British Airways *(www.britishairways.com)* and Air New Zealand *(www.airnewzealand.com)* operate regular flights to Auckland, Wellington and Christchurch. Flight times vary from around 27–34 hours depending on the carrier and where you stop en route. Since 2011 Air New Zealand has been operating its much praised 'Skycouch' in the Economy Class on long-haul flights. A row of three seats can be turned into a bed-like space with footrests being raised to fill the gap with the seats in front. Two adults pay the normal price, the third seat is about half the price – an investment that is worth looking into on such a long flight.

RESPONSIBLE TRAVEL

It doesn't take a lot to be environmentally friendly whilst travelling. Don't just think about your carbon footprint whilst flying to and from your holiday destination but also about how you can protect nature and culture abroad. As a tourist it is especially important to respect nature, look out for local products, cycle instead of driving, save water and much more. If you would like to find out more about eco-tourism please visit: *www.ecotourism.org*

Singapore Airlines *(www.singaporeair. com)* operates one of the fastest eastern routes with a short stopover in Singapore. Qantas (www.qantas.com) has competitive prices and excellent service but lands in both Singapore and Australia first. If you want to divide your flight time into 6–7 hour legs (Dubai, Singapore, Sydney), then check out Emirates *(www.emirates. com)*. Tip: flights to Australia are often relatively cheap. You can then travel on to New Zealand using a budget airline such as Virgin Australia *(www.virgin australia.com)* or Jetstar *(www.jetstar. com)*. But reckon with delays, onward flights from different terminals, costs for excess baggage, etc. No-frills airlines have a baggage allowance of just 20kg, international airlines normally 23kg, Emirates 30kg. Air Asia *(www.airasia. com)* is a low budget airline, that since 2011 flies to Christchurch from Paris and London via Kuala Lumpur. For problems with excess luggage see *www.packsend. co.nz* and *www.got-excess-baggage.com*. Baggage allowances can be compared on *www.luggagelimits.com*.

The minimum age in New Zealand to be able to rent a car is 21. An 'as new' medium category car costs approx. 80 NZ$/day *(e.g. Maui | Richard Pearse Dr. | Mangere | Auckland | tel. 09 2 75 30 13 | www.maui-rentals.com)* plus fully comprehensive insurance *(approx. 15–30 NZ$/day)*. Older models are cheaper. Reductions are offered for a rental period of more than 3 weeks. Certains routes are not covered by rental car insurance. Don't save on your insurance

From arrival to weather

Holiday from start to finish: the most important addresses and information for your trip to New Zealand

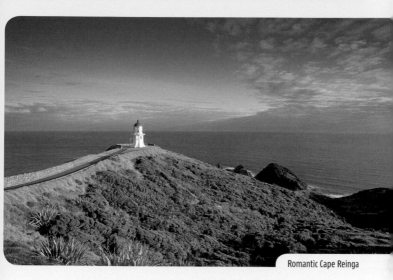

Romantic Cape Reinga

coverage – if you do, check your credit limit. Some rental companies charge a 5000 NZ$ deposit, payable immediately, if you do not opt for a fully comprehensive insurance.

Incl. fully comprehensive insurance *(approx. 60 NZ$)* and campsite charges *(approx. 40 NZ$)*, a 1–2-year-old campervan sleeping 2 (without shower/WC) costs around 250 NZ$/day between Feb–April. Older vehicles are some 20–30% cheaper. Additional information for those with tents or in a campervan can also be found under *www.goseenewzealand.co.nz* and *www.camping.org.nz*.

CLIMATE, WHEN TO GO

The best time is Nov/Dec (spring) and Feb, March, April (summer/autumn) when the weather is generally more stable. It is however always windy. On average, rainfall is between 700–1500 ml which is why the vegetation is so lush. The climate on South Island is similar to than in Central Europe; the north of North Island is more sub-tropical. Perfect winter sport conditions on North and South Island can be found in July–Sept. Whenever you travel, a warm pullover and rainproof clothing are a must. For more about the weather, see: *www.metservice.com*.

CUSTOMS

Items for personal use may be brought with you duty free, as can presents worth not more than 700 NZ$, 250g tobacco, 2.2L spirits, 4.5L wine or beer. Perishable food may not be brought in (be warned: stiff fines! *www.customs.govt.nz*). For allowances when returning to the UK, see: *www.hmrc.gov.uk/customs/arriving/arrivingnoneu.htm*

DRIVING

New Zealanders drive on the left, are defensive drivers and, thanks to low traffic

CURRENCY CONVERTER

£	NZ$	NZ$	£
1	2	1	0.50
3	6	3	1.50
5	10	5	2.50
13	26	13	6.50
40	80	40	20
75	150	75	37.50
120	240	120	60
250	500	250	125
500	1000	500	250

$	NZ$	NZ$	$
1	1.20	1	0.85
3	3.60	3	2.50
5	6	5	4.20
13	15.60	13	11
40	48	40	33
75	90	75	62.50
120	144	120	100
250	300	250	210
500	600	500	420

For current exchange rates see www.xe.com

density, driving is not stressful. Main roads (State Highways – SH – and Highways – Hwy – in this guidebook) are tarmaced and well built but often very twisty, which means journeys can often take much longer. Roads with several lanes are only found around major cities. The maximum speed limit is 100km/h (60mph), in built-up areas 50km/h (30mph). Speed cameras are used extensively. Breath tests are frequent (limit: 0.4). At roundabouts, give way to traffic coming from the right. Until

March 2012 this also applied at normal junctions. An international driving licence is required that is only valid in combination with the licence of the country you come from. Telephoning when driving is only allowed with a hands-free mobile phone system.

ELECTRICITY

230V. 3 flat pin plugs only are used in New Zealand. An adapter, available at local electricians and luggage shops, is needed.

EMBASSIES & CONSULATES

BRITISH HIGH COMMISSION
44 Hill St. | Wellington 6011 | tel. +46 4 924 2888 | ukinnewzealand.fco.gov.uk

CONSULATE GENERAL OF THE US
3rd Floor, Citigroup Building | 23 Customs St. (cnr. Commerce St) | Auckland 1010 | tel. +46 9 303 2724 ext: 2800 | newzealand. usembassy.gov

HIGH COMMISSION OF CANADA
Level 11, 125 The Terrace | Wellington 6011 | tel. +46 4 473 9577 | www.canadainter national.gc.ca/new_zealand-nouvelle_ zelande/offices-bureaux/hc_info

IMMIGRATION

No visa is required for Australian citizens with a valid passport. UK citizens (and other British passport holders with the right to reside permanently in the UK) may stay for up to 6 months. Citizens of EU member states: 3 months. Citizens of countries which have a visa waiver agreement with New Zealand (incl. US and Canada) can stay up to three months. Passports must be valid for at least 3 months beyond the date of your return (as marked on your plane ticket). For stu-dent intending to work temporarily in New Zealand see: *www.workandincome. govt.nz*.

INFORMATION

The New Zealand tourist information maintains an informative website: *www. newzealand.com*. *www.tourism.net.nz* also provides useful tips and addresses.

INTERNET CAFÉS & WI-FI

Internet cafés are on every corner in tourist centres and all 4 and 5-star hotels have Internet connections in rooms (generally charged separately). The many i-SITEs (visitor information) have Internet connections for guests. If you have a mobile phone or notebook with a Wi-Fi connection you can use the hotspots in around 600 cafés, campsites and hotels – virtually always free of charge (your browser will tell you). Ipass *(www.ipass.com)*, Telecom New Zealand *(www.telecom. co.nz/wirelesshotspot)* or the popular CaféNET *(www.cafenet.co.nz)* offer Wi-Fi prepaid cards. Hotspots can be found under: *www.jiwire.com*, *www.wi-fihot spotsdirectory.com*, *www.wififreespot. com*, *www.totalhotspots.com (only ipass Wi-Fi Service)*

HEALTH

No inoculations are necessary. Medical care in comparable to that in the UK. A travel health insurance with return transport option should be taken out. Tourists benefit from free initial treatment in the case of an accident.

MONEY & CREDIT CARDS

Visa and Eurocard/Mastercard are accepted virtually everywhere, especially at petrol stations, in most supermarkets and hotels. Credit cards can be used to obtain cash from dispensers (with the Maestro sign) as can EC cards with PIN (cheaper). A 2% surcharge is being increasingly levied when payment is made with a credit card (garages, car hire companies). Travellers' cheques are still a safe alternative.

NEWSPAPERS & MAGAZINES

European newspapers and magazines appear on the shelves 1–2 weeks after publication, if at all. The selection of papers in New Zealand is large in relation to its population.

OPENING HOURS

Since the Shops Closing Act has been amended, many supermarkets are open until late in the evening and at weekends. Most shops are generally open from 9am–5.30pm, late night shopping on Thu or Fri is until 8pm. Shops are also open in the larger cities on Sun from 11am–4pm.

PHONE & MOBILE PHONE

Local calls from private phones are toll free. Phone cards available form dairies and newsagents are needed for public phones. Cards for private phone companies are cheaper and available in most internet cafés everywhere.

Calls to Europe cost approx. 5p/min. Roaming fees for mobile phones are generally expensive. If staying for a longer period it may be better to divert all mobile calls to your mailbox before departure and then buy a prepaid chip for your mobile in New Zealand, e.g. from Vodafone (40 NZ$ incl. 10 NZ$ credit). You will then have a New Zealand

BUDGETING

Coffee	£2/$3
	for a café au lait
Souvenirs	from approx. £35/$55
	for a jade tiki
Wine	£4/$6
	for a glass of wine
Fish & chips	£3½/$5½
	for one helping
Petrol	85p/$1¼
	for 1 litre super
Bus fare	approx. £35/$55
	one way, from
	Auckland–Wellington

mobile number and a voice mailbox. Rates/min.: 1.39–1.99 NZ$ for a call to the UK (7am–7pm).

The international dialling code to the UK is *0044*, US/Canada *001*, to New Zealand *0046*. *0800* numbers listed in this guidebook are toll free within New Zealand. In case of emergency dial *111*.

POST

A postcard to Europe or North America costs 1.90 NZ$ and takes around 6–10 days. A letter costs 2.40 NZ$.

TIME

New Zealand is close to the International Dateline. During the UK summer, New Zealand is 11 hours ahead of GMT; between Oct–early April 13 hours. For sunrise and sunset times etc. see: *www.timeanddate.com*.

TIPPING

Tipping is not standard practice – even if this rule is being ignored more and more when the service is really good.

TRANSPORT IN NEW ZEALAND

Trains only run between Auckland and Wellington, Picton and Christchurch and between Christchurch and Greymouth *(TranzAlpine | www.railnewzea land.com)*. Buses (coaches) operate a regular service between all towns on North and South Island. They are reliable and the perfect means of transport for backpackers.

Passes for buses, trains, ferries and planes are especially reasonable, e.g. Flexi Pass or hop-on-hop-off tickets *(www.intercity coach.co.nz and www.flexi trips.co.nz)* and Scenic Rail Pass *(www.tranzscenic.co.nz)*. Backpacker buses operated by Magic *(www.magicbus.co.nz)* and Kiwi Experience *(www.kiwiexperience.com)* are cheaper still. All passes can also be bought on the spot.

Inland flights are available through Air New Zealand *(tel. 0800 73 70 00 | www. airnewzealand.com)* and the Qantas subsidiary Jetstar *(tel. 0800 80 09 95 | www. jetstar.com)*. See the Internet for special rates. A return flight Auckland–Christchurch costs approx. 160 NS$, depending on the departure time.

For campervan drivers: book ferries between North and South Island for the Nov–March period in advance from home, or shortly after arrival. *Tel. 0064 44 98 30 00 | www.interislander.co.nz or www. bluebridge.co.nz*

WHERE TO STAY

If you're looking for somwhere to stay, check out *www.superiorinns.co.nz, www. heritageinns.co.nz, www.nzcamping. co.nz, www.friars.co.nz or www.bnb.co.nz*. Very reasonable hotel rates can be found

4 weeks before your date of arrival under *www.wotif.co.nz*, *www.ratestogo.com* and *www.fourcorners.co.nz*. Backpackers can find useful tip under *www.backpack. co.nz*, *www.vip.co.nz* and *www.yha.org.nz*. 'Tourist flats' (with a certain level of comfort) and cabins (basic) on campsites cost approx. 40 NZ$ per person; 25 NZ$ is the average price in one of the many backpacker hostels in a dormitory or double room.

A pitch on one of the generally well-equipped campsites costs 35 NZ$ per night for 2 people and a campervan. The some 200 'Conservation Campsites' run by the Department of Conservation (DOC) are in romantic locations but without any degree of comfort. Note: a new law

passed in 2011 restricts so-called 'freedom camping' (i.e. not in campsites) especially for vehicles without a WC. The reason: too much pollution in the countryside from inconsiderate campers.

Various hotel chains *(Best Western, Golden Chain, Flag)* and agencies (Main Stay) offer hotel passes *(120–190 NZ$ per room/ night)*. *Rural Holidays | Christchurch | tel. 03 3 55 62 18 | www.ruralholidays.co.nz |* or *www.nzfarmholidays.co.nz*, *www.rural tourism.co.nz* and *www.nzhomestay.co.nz* arrange stays on farms. Rooms/cabins and flats often consist of one or two bedrooms, a kitchenette incl. microwave, etc. that can help keep costs down. The average price for a modern 1-bedroomed flat is 130–170 NZ$ per night.

WEATHER IN WELLINGTON

	Jan	Feb	March	April	May	June	July	Aug	Sept	Oct	Nov	Dec
Daytime temperatures in °C/°F	21/70	21/70	19/66	17/63	14/57	13/55	12/54	12/54	14/57	16/61	17/63	19/66
Nighttime temperatures in °C/°F	13/55	13/55	12/54	11/52	8/46	7/45	6/43	6/43	8/46	9/48	10/50	12/54
Sunshine hours/day	8	7	6	5	4	4	4	4	6	6	7	7
Precipitation days/month	7	4	5	10	11	14	14	15	10	10	11	10
Water temperatures in °C/°F	17/63	18/64	18/64	17/63	14/57	14/57	13/55	13/55	12/54	14/57	14/57	17/63

NOTES

FOR YOUR NEXT HOLIDAY ...

MARCO POLO TRAVEL GUIDES

- PACKED WITH INSIDER TIPS
- BEST WALKS AND TOURS
- FULL-COLOUR PULL-OUT MAP
  AND STREET ATLAS

ROAD ATLAS

The green line ▬▬ indicates the Trips & Tours (p. 106–111)
The blue line ▬▬ indicates The perfect route (p. 30–31)

All tours are also marked on the pull-out map

Photo: Purakaunui Falls, South Island

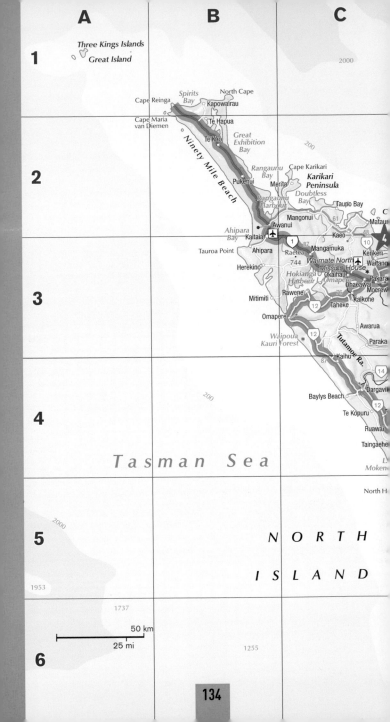

A

1
Three Kings Islands
° ᴗ Great Island
2000

B

1
Spirits
Bay
North Cape
Cape Reinga
Kapowairau
Cape Maria
van Diemen
Te Hapua
Great
Exhibition
Bay
Te Kao

2
Rangaunu
Bay
Cape Karikari
Pukenui
Merita
Karikari
Peninsula
Doubtless
Bay
Taupo Bay
Rangaunu
Harbour
Mangonui
61
Awanui
Ahipara
Bay
Kaitaia
Kaeo
10
Kerikeri
Tauroa Point
Ahipara
Raetea
87
Mangamuka
Waitang
Herekino
744
Waimate North
Mission House
Pakara
Hokianga
Harbour
Okaihau
Omapere
Ohaeawai
Moerew
Rawene
Kaikohe
Mitimiti
76
Taheke
Omapere
12
Awarua
Waipoua
Kauri Forest
12
Tutamoe Ra.
Paraka
87
Kaihu
14
Baylys Beach
Dargavil
Te Kopuru
12
Ruawai
Taingaehe
L.
Moken

3

4
Ninety Mile Beach

T a s m a n   S e a

200

C

1
2000

2
200
Cape Karikari
Matau
C
48

5
North H

N O R T H

I S L A N D

6
2000

1953

1737

50 km
25 mi

1255

134

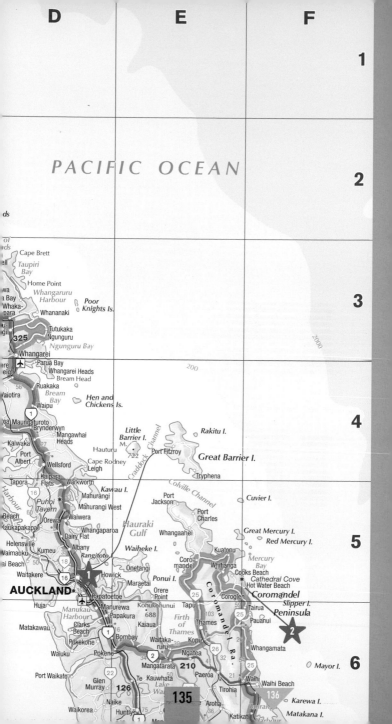

Grid references

D **E** **F**

1

2

3

4

5

6

PACIFIC OCEAN

ds

of
ds
Cape Brett
*Taupiri
Bay*
ell
wa
a Bay
Whaka-
para
Home Point
*Whangaruru
Harbour*
Whananaki
*Poor
Knights Is.*
ug
gi
325
Tutukaka
Ngunguru
Ngunguru Bay
Whangarei
re
eigh
Parua Bay
Whangarei Heads
Bream Head
Ruakaka
*Bream
Bay*
*Hen and
Chickens Is.*
aiotira
Waipu
Maungaturoto
Brynderwyn
Mangawhai
Heads
Kaiwaka
Port
Albert
Wellsford
*Little
Barrier I.*
M.
Hauturu 722
Craddock Channel
Rakitu I.
Great Barrier I.
Kaipara
Flats
Cape Rodney
Leigh
Warkworth
Port Fitzroy
Tapora
Harbour
*Puhoi
Tavern*
Kawau I.
Mahurangi
Mahurangi West
Colville Channel
Tryphena
Beach
kaukapakapa
Orewa
Waiwera
Whangaparoa
*Hauraki
Gulf*
Port
Jackson
Port
Charles
Cuvier I.
Helensville
Waimauku
ai Beach
Waitakere
Kumeu
Dairy Flat
Albany
Rangitoto
Waiheke I.
Whangaahei
Coro-
mandel
Whitianga
Kuatonu
Great Mercury I.
Red Mercury I.
*Mercury
Bay*
Cooks Beach
Cathedral Cove
Hot Water Beach
Howick
Onetangi
Ponui I.
AUCKLAND
Papatoetoe
Maraetai
Orere
Point
Coroglen
**Coromandel
Peninsula**
Huia
*Manukau
Harbour*
Manurewa
Papakura
Kohukohunui
688
Tapu
25
*Firth
of
Thames*
103
Slipper I.
Tairua
Pauanui
Matakawau
Clarks
Beach
Kaiaua
Thames
Pukekohe
Bombay
6
Waitaka-
ruru
Kopu
26
Whangamata
Waiuku
Pokeno
Ngatea
210
O Mayor I.
Port Waikato
22
Glen
Murray
Te Kauwhata
Mangatarata
Paeroa
Waihi
Waihi Beach
126
Lake
Tirohia
136
Karewa I.
Waikorea
Naike
Huntly
Aroha
Katikati
Matakana I.

135

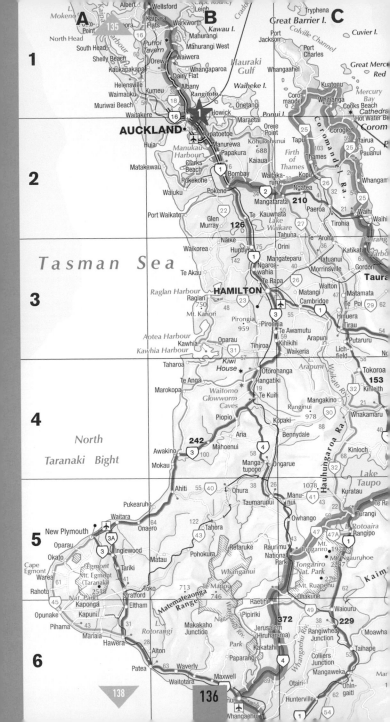

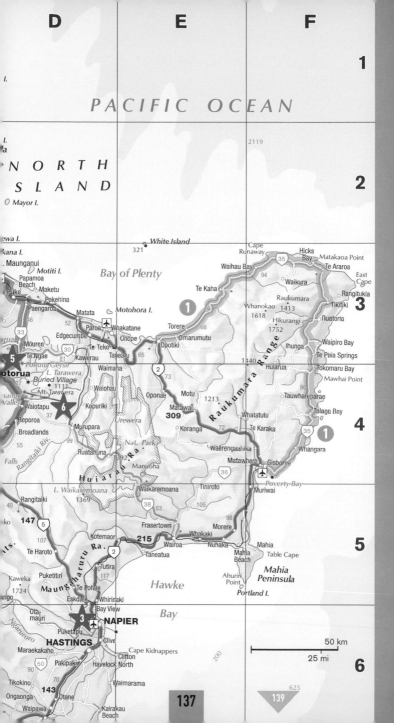

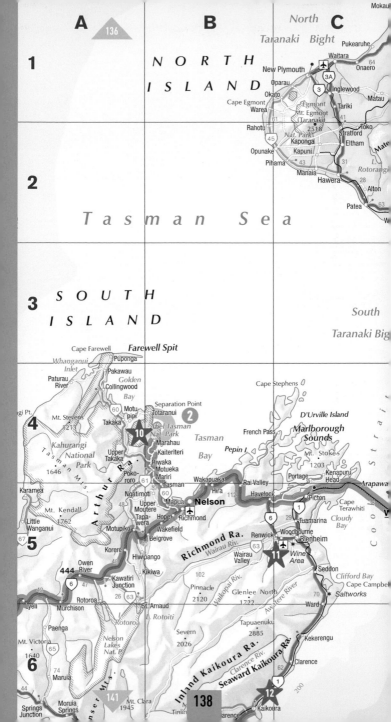

North
Taranaki Bight

Mokau

Pukearuhe

Waitara

New Plymouth

64
Onaero

A 136

B

C

1

N O R T H

I S L A N D

Oparau

3A

Okato

3

Inglewood

Matau

Cape Egmont
Warea

Egmont
Mt. Egmont
(Taranaki)
2518
Nat. Park

Tariki

41

Toko

Rahotu

45

Kapongai

Stratford

Eltham

Mate

2

Opunake

Kapuni

43

Manaia

31

Rotorang

28

Pihama

Hawera

Alton

T a s m a n   S e a

Patea

63

W

3

S O U T H

I S L A N D

South

Taranaki Big

Cape Farewell

Farewell Spit

Whanganui
Inlet

Puponga

Paturau
River

Pakawau

Cape Stephens

Collingwood

Golden
Bay

60
Motu-
pipi

Separation Point
Totaranui

2

D'Urville Island

gi Pt.

Mt. Stevens
1213

Takaka

10

Abel Tasman
Nat. Park

Marahau

French Pass

Marlborough
Sounds

4

Kahurangi
National
Park

Upper
Takaka

Kaiteriteri

Riwaka

Tasman
Bay

Pepin I.

Mt. Stokes
1203

Kenapuru
Head

Portage

Karamea

1646

Poko-
roro

61

Motueka
Mariri

Tasman

Wakapuaka

Hira

Rai Valley

Havelock

Arapawa

Noatimoti

60

Mapua

Nelson

Picton

Cape
Terawhiti

Mt. Kendall
1762

Upper
Moutere

Hope

Richmond

1

Tuamarina

Cloudy
Bay

Little
Wanganui

Tapa-
wera

Wakefield

6

Woodbourne

29

5

67

Motupiko

Belgrove

Richmond Ra.

63

Renwick

11

Blenheim

Wine
Area

444

Owen
River

Korere

40

Hiwipango

Wairau Riv.

Wairau
Valley

Seddon

Clifford Bay

6

47

Kawatiri
Junction

Kikiwa

102

Waikopai Riv.

Glenlee North
1722

70

Cape Campbe

Saltworks

Lyell

Rotoroa

26

63

St. Arnaud

Pinnacle
2120

Awatere River

Ward

Murchison

L. Rotoiti

L.
Rotoroa

Severn
2026

Tapuaenuku
2885

Kekerengu

Paenga

Nelson
Lakes
Nat.

Mt. Victoria
1640

65

Clarence

6

44

Maruia

74

Mt. Clara
1945

Inland Kaikoura Ra.

Clarence River

1

62

200

Springs
Junction

Moruia
Springs

141

nser Mts.

Tinlin

138

Clarence

Seaward Kaikoura Ra.

12

Kaikoura

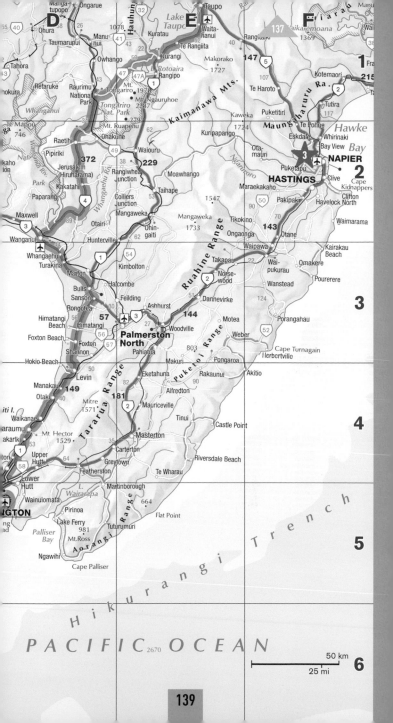

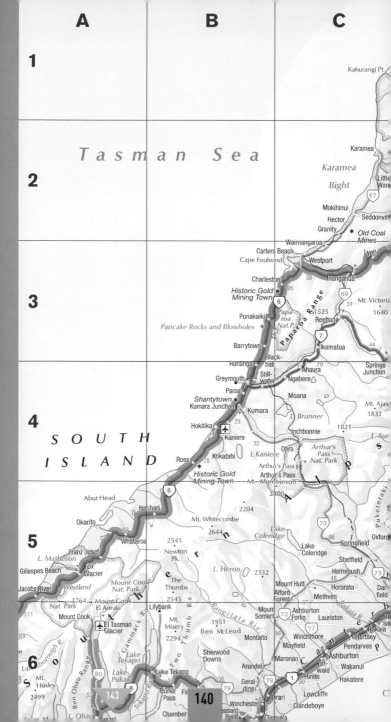

A **B** **C**

1

Kahurangi Pt.

Tasman Sea

Karamea

Karamea
Bight

2

Little Wan

67

Mokihinui
Hector   Seddonvil
Granity
Waimangaroa   Old Coal
Carters Beach   Mines
Cape Foulwind   Westport   Lyell
Charleston   38   Inangahua
Historic Gold   95
Mining Town   6

3

Papa-
roa   69
.1525   Range   31   Mt. Victoria
Punakaiki   Reefton   1640
Nat.P.
Pancake Rocks and Blowholes   7
Barrytown   Ikamatua   44
Black-   79   Springs
Runanga   ball   Ahaura   Junction
Greymouth   Still-   Ngahere
Paroa   water
Shantytown   Moana
Kumara Junction   Kumara   L Brunner   Mt. Ajax
Hokitika   23   Inchbonnie   1832
Kaniere   82   1821   L. Sur

4

S O U T H

Kokatahi   Otira   Arthur's
Ross   78   L Kaniere   Pass
Historic Gold   Arthur's Pass   Nat. Park
I S L A N D   *Mining Town*   Mt. Murchinson
6   2400
Abut Head   2204   73   Puke
Harihari   Mt. Whitecombe   Lake
Okarito   2644   Coleridge   96   Oxford
Franz Josef   Lake   Springfield
L. Matheson   Whataroa   2545   Coleridge
Fox   Newton   Sheffield
Gillespes Beach   Glacier   Pk.   L. Heron   2332   Homebush   73
Jacobs River   *Westland*   The   Mount Hutt   Hororata   Dar-
Mount Cook   Thumbs   Alford   Methven   field
3764   *Nat. Park*   2545   Forest   47
Mount Cook   El Aoraki   Lilybank   Mount   Ashburton   Lauriston   Rakaia
El Tasman   Mt.   *Rangitata Ri*   Somers   72   Forks   Chertsey
Glacier   Misery   1951   Winchmore   77   Pendarves
Ben McLeod   Mayfield   Ashburton
Lake   2294   Maronan   Tin-   Wakanui
Mt.   Tekapo   Sherwood   wald
Huxley   80   Downs   Arundel   1   Hinds   Hakatere
2499   Lake   Lake Tekapo   Geral-   79   50   Lowcliffe
Puka   56   dine   Orari   Clandeboye
Burke   79   Pleasant
Pass   Point   Temuka
Chamber

143   140

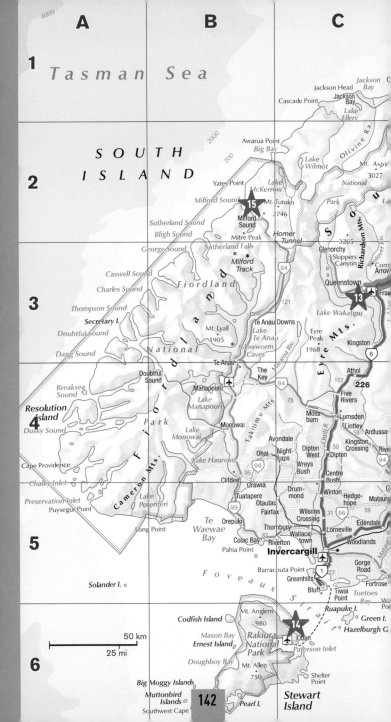

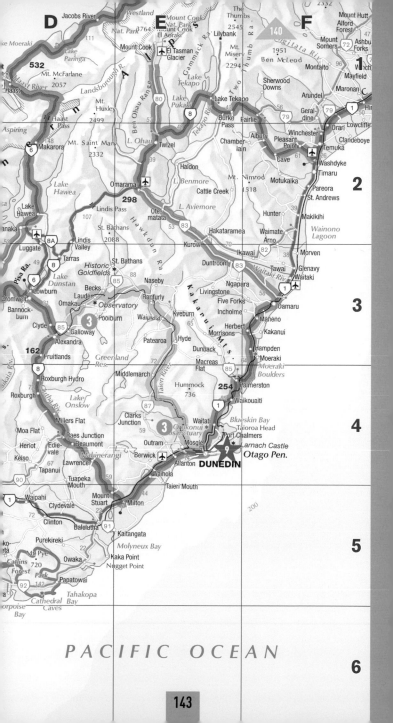

PACIFIC OCEAN

KEY TO ROAD ATLAS

Highway, multilane divided road - under construction Autobahn, mehrspurige Straße - in Bau	═══ ═ ═ ═	Autoroute, route à plusieurs voies - en construction Autosnelweg, weg met meer rijstroken - in aanleg
Trunk road - under construction Fernverkehrsstraße - in Bau	─── ─ ─ ─	Route à grande circulation - en construction Weg voor interlokaal verkeer - in aanleg
Principal highway Hauptstraße		Route principale Hoofdweg
Secondary road Nebenstraße		Route secondaire Overige verharde wegen
Practicable road, track Fahrweg, Piste		Chemin carrossable, piste Weg, piste
Road numbering Straßennummerierung	E20 11 70 26 5 40 9	Numérotage des routes Wegnummering
Distances in kilometers Entfernungen in Kilometer	**259** 130 129	Distances en kilomètres Afstand in kilometers
Height in meters - Pass Höhe in Meter - Pass	1365 •	Altitude en mètres - Col Hoogte in meters - Pas
Railway - Railway ferry Eisenbahn - Eisenbahnfähre	───── ··········	Chemin de fer - Ferry-boat Spoorweg - Spoorpont
Car ferry - Shipping route Autofähre - Schifffahrtslinie		Bac autos - Ligne maritime Autoveer - Scheepvaartlijn
Major international airport - Airport Wichtiger internationaler Flughafen - Flughafen	✈ ✈	Aéroport importante international - Aéroport Belangrijke internationale luchthaven - Luchthaven
International boundary - Province boundary Internationale Grenze - Provinzgrenze		Frontière internationale - Limite de Province Internationale grens - Provinciale grens
Undefined boundary Unbestimmte Grenze		Frontière d'Etat non définie Rijksgrens onbepaalt
Time zone boundary Zeitzonengrenze	-4h Greenwich Time ••••••••• -3h Greenwich Time	Limite de fuseau horaire Tijdzone-grens
National capital Hauptstadt eines souveränen Staates	**MANILA**	Capitale nationale Hoofdstad van een souvereine staat
Federal capital Hauptstadt eines Bundesstaates	**Kuching**	Capitale d'un état fédéral Hoofdstad van een deelstat
Restricted area Sperrgebiet		Zone interdite Verboden gebied
National park Nationalpark		Parc national Nationaal park
Ancient monument Antikes Baudenkmal	∴	Monument antiques Antiek monument
Interesting cultural monument Sehenswertes Kulturdenkmal	★ Angkor Wat	Monument culturel interéssant Bezienswaardig cultuurmonument
Interesting natural monument Sehenswertes Naturdenkmal	★ Ha Long Bay	Monument naturel interéssant Bezienswaardig natuurmonument
Well Brunnen	⌣	Puits Bron
Trips & Tours Ausflüge & Touren		Excursions & tours Uitstapjes & tours
Perfect route Perfekte Route		Itinéraire idéal Perfecte route
MARCO POLO Highlight	★1	MARCO POLO Highlight

INDEX

This index lists all places, sights and beaches in this guide.
Numbers in bold indicate a main entry.

CREDITS

WRITE TO US

e-mail: info@marcopologuides.co.uk

Did you have a great holiday?
Is there something on your mind?
Whatever it is, let us know!
Whether you want to praise, alert us
to errors or give us a personal tip –
MARCO POLO would be pleased to
hear from you.
We do everything we can to provide the
very latest information for your trip.

Nevertheless, despite all of our authors'
thorough research, errors can creep in.
MARCO POLO does not accept any
liability for this. Please contact us by
e-mail or post.

MARCO POLO Travel Publishing Ltd
Pinewood, Chineham Business Park
Crockford Lane, Chineham
Basingstoke, Hampshire RG24 8AL
United Kingdom

PICTURE CREDITS
Cover photograph: Queen Charlotte Sound, Laif: Akhtar
DuMont Bildarchiv: Emmler (3 top, 3 bottom, 18/19, 26 left, 30 right, 52/53, 66, 77, 88, 101, 106/107, 116/117, 120), Schröder/Schwarzbach (57, 62, 74, 92, 95, 115); F. M. Frei (22/23, 122 top); R. Gerth (30 left, 60/61, 123, 125); Getty Images/FoodPix: Hagiwara (26 right); Getty Images/Gallo Images: Delimont (87, 111); Getty Images/Lonely Planet: Blakers (9); Mike Grobelny/AUT University (17 top); hoopnotica (16 centre); Lade: BAV (front flap left, 105); Laif: Akhtar (1 top), Emmler (3 centre, 12/13, 21, 27, 37, 46, 49, 65, 79, 80, 90, 108, 112/113, 119, 121, 122 bottom), Hauser (2 bottom, 10/11, 24/25, 28, 28/29, 29, 40, 50, 54, 68/69, 98/99, 145), Heeb (5, 15, 43, 82/83, 120/121, 132/133), Kristensen (34); H. Leue (2 centre bottom, 32/33, 38); Look: age fotostock (70); mauritius images: Alamy (7, 8, 44, 73, 84/85), Delimont/Williford (103), Raga (2 centre top, 6), Vidler (2 top, 4); Renaissance Brewing Company (16 top), vario imagebroker: imagebroker (front flap right, 58, 96/97); Justin Westgate (16 bottom); Woodlyn Park: Billy Black (17 bottom)

1st Edition 2013
Worldwide Distribution: Marco Polo Travel Publishing Ltd, Pinewood, Chineham Business Park,
Crockford Lane, Basingstoke, Hampshire RG24 8AL, United Kingdom. Email: sales@marcopolouk.com
© MAIRDUMONT GmbH & Co. KG, Ostfildern
Chief editor: Marion Zorn
Authors: Bruni Gebauer, Stefan Huy; editor: Christina Sothmann
Programme supervision: Anita Dahlinger, Ann-Katrin Kutzner, Nikolai Michaelis
Picture editors: Gabriele Forst, Stefan Scholtz
What's hot: wunder media, Munich
Cartography road atlas & pull-out map: © MAIRDUMONT, Ostfildern
Design: milchhof : atelier, Berlin; Front cover, pull-out map cover, page 1: factor product munich
Translated from German by Christopher Wynne; editor of the English edition: Christopher Wynne
Prepress: M. Feuerstein, Wigel

DOS & DON'TS

A few tips to make your visit to New Zealand easier

DON'T PLAN TOO MANY STOPS EN ROUTE

Don't be tempted to break your journey to New Zealand for too long. The number of inviting places to visit en route on your trip half way round the world is huge, but you'll need a lot of time in New Zealand itself. You should plan at least three to four weeks for a tour of North and South Islands.

DON'T GIVE IN TO JETLAG

Avoid high-protein (energy-giving) food on the plane. Drink a lot on the flight – but steer clear of alcohol. In this way you can deal with the jetlag problem, which upsets the body's internal rhythm, much better. When you arrive in New Zealand don't go to bed until the evening and after a light meal. This will help you adjust to the new daily rhythm.

KEEP OUT OF THE SUN!

The risk of skin cancer down under is not something to be taken lightly. The intensity of the sun's rays close to the hole in the ozone layer is dangerous. Always apply suncream with a high protection factor to your skin. Wear sunglasses, something on your head with a wide brim and cover your shoulders and arms whenever outside. And don't forget: on and in the water the sun's rays are particularly aggessive!

DON'T DRINK WATER FROM RIVERS

More than half of the lakes and rivers in the national parks are infected by the Giardia parasite. Don't drink from streams or leap into certain stretches of water. The parasite passes through the mouth into the stomach and intestines and, after around 3 weeks, causes diarrhea, excess gas and abdominal cramps. Medical treatment is successful and swift. Boil water when out in the countryside before drinking it or use chemical purifiers (e.g. transportable filtration devices – Giardia rated filters – or tablets). When in the back of beyond, answer the call of nature away from any source of water and cover everything with earth. But don't then wash your hands in a river or lake. Use a bowl instead and tip the water away on the ground.

Didymo (or rock snot), a dangerous algae, is also a major problem that has now spread to most bodies of water in New Zealand. Make sure you remove all traces of algae from anything that was in the water before entering any other river or lake (information under *www.biosecurity.govt.nz*).

DON'T MUDDLE HOTEL WITH MOTEL

In New Zealand many pubs call themselves hotels – and only have basic accommodation (pub beds) if at all, which most tourists would rather avoid. It's better to ask for a motel if you're looking for somewhere to stay the night.